# TRANSFORMATIVE COLLABORATION

## Five Commitments for Leading a Professional Learning Community

Tonia Flanagan

Gavin Grift

Kylie Lipscombe

Colin Sloper

Janelle Wills

*Foreword by Alma Harris and Michelle Jones*

Solution Tree | Press

a division of
Solution Tree

American version published in the United States by Solution Tree Press

555 North Morton Street
Bloomington, IN 47404
800.733.6786 (toll free) / 812.336.7700
FAX: 812.336.7790

email: info@SolutionTree.com

SolutionTree.com

Visit **go.SolutionTree.com/PLCbooks** to download the free reproducibles in this book.

Printed in the United States of America

Library of Congress Cataloging-in-Publication Data

Names: Flanagan, Tonia, author.
Title: Transformative collaboration : five commitments for leading a
   professional learning community / Tonia Flanagan, Gavin Grift, Kylie
   Lipscombe, Colin Sloper, Janelle Wills ; foreword by Alma Harris and
   Michelle Jones.
Description: Bloomington, IN : Solution Tree Press, 2021. | Includes
   bibliographical references and index.
Identifiers: LCCN 2020050679 (print) | LCCN 2020050680 (ebook) | ISBN
   9781951075996 (paperback) | ISBN 9781947604377 (ebook)
Subjects: LCSH: Professional learning communities. | Teachers--Professional
   relationships. | School improvement programs.
Classification: LCC LB1731 .F535 2021  (print) | LCC LB1731  (ebook) | DDC
   371.2/07--dc23
LC record available at https://lccn.loc.gov/2020050679
LC ebook record available at https://lccn.loc.gov/2020050680

**Solution Tree**
Jeffrey C. Jones, CEO
Edmund M. Ackerman, President

**Solution Tree Press**
*President and Publisher:* Douglas M. Rife
*Associate Publisher:* Sarah Payne-Mills

*Art Director:* Rian Anderson
*Managing Production Editor:* Kendra Slayton
*Copy Chief:* Jessi Finn
*Production Editor:* Miranda Addonizio
*Content Development Specialist:* Amy Rubenstein
*Proofreader:* Kate St. Ives
*Text and Cover Designer:* Rian Anderson
*Editorial Assistants:* Sarah Ludwig and Elijah Oates

**Transformative Collaboration: Five Commitments for Leading a Professional Learning Community** was
originally published in Australia by Hawker Brownlow Education

© 2016 by Hawker Brownlow Education

# TABLE OF CONTENTS

## CHAPTER 4
## SHAPE SCHOOL STRUCTURES FOR SUCCESS ...................................... 55

# ABOUT THE AUTHORS

**Tonia Flanagan** is former director of the Centre for Professional Learning. She currently serves as a senior training associate for Hawker Brownlow Education and a primary school principal. With over thirty years of experience in education as a teacher, regional curriculum advisor, school principal and consultant, Tonia has expertise in instructional leadership and how it can have a direct impact on student achievement.

An experienced teacher-educator, Tonia has successfully led the development of PLCs in a systemwide approach within over forty primary and secondary schools. She has facilitated workshops for education leaders on contemporary learning, school improvement, data analysis, building collaborative school cultures, and adaptive leadership.

**Gavin Grift** is the founder and CEO of Grift Education. Gavin's passion, commitment, humor, and highly engaging style have made him one of Australia's most in-demand presenters. Through his keynotes, seminars, and coaching services, Gavin connects with international audiences on how to cultivate authentic collaboration, build success in others, and genuinely commit to reflective practice. His belief in the development of defined professional autonomy for educators challenges and connects the heads and hearts of his audience members.

Gavin has held numerous educational leadership positions, including serving as a cluster educator, leading teacher, assistant principal, and director of professional learning. He also served as the executive director of Hawker Brownlow Professional Learning Solutions and the managing director of Solution Tree Australia.

Gavin serves as a training associate for Thinking Collaborative's Cognitive Coaching Seminars® and Professional Learning Communities (PLCs) at Work®. He is also the cofounder of the Centre of Learning Architects, in support of both teachers and leaders becoming students of their own professional practice.

Gavin is coauthor of numerous articles and books, including *Collaborative Teams That Transform Schools: The Next Step in PLCs* (Marzano, Heflebower, Hoegh, Warrick, & Grift, 2016), and the second edition of *Teachers as Architects of Learning: Twelve Constructs to Design and Configure Successful Learning Experiences* (Grift & Major, 2018). Most recently, he worked with Colin Sloper to revise *Learning by Doing: A Handbook for Professional Learning Communities at Work* (DuFour, DuFour, Eaker, Many, & Mattos, 2016) for the Australian context. He has led the development of PLC networks across Australia, culminating in the establishment of the Centre for Professional Learning Communities. He is committed to growing the legacy of Richard and Rebecca DuFour's work through the PLC at Work process, which has been transforming schools in Australia since its pilot program launched in Adelaide, Melbourne, and Canberra in 2010. To learn more about Gavin's work, visit www.grifteducation.com.

**Kylie Lipscombe, PhD,** is a senior lecturer, researcher, and associate academic program director of postgraduate studies in educational leadership at the University of Wollongong, New South Wales, Australia. She is also president of the New South Wales branch of the Australian Council of Educational Leaders. With twenty years of experience in education organizations, she has supported the implementation of PLCs within a variety of Australian education systems and schools. Dr. Lipscombe is adept at guiding schools through the rigorous process of reculturing as a PLC, acting as a school-based critical friend and coach along the way.

Dr. Lipscombe has led the implementation of improvements to teaching and learning in a variety of education sectors. She has been an education consultant, a literacy project officer and coach, a lecturer, an assistant principal, and a classroom teacher. As a lead writer in national curriculum projects, she has developed a deep understanding of curriculum planning and implementation.

As an experienced education researcher, Dr. Lipscombe has served on various research projects. Her master's degree in education explored how reflective and inquiry dialogue can improve team capacity and her doctorate focused on digital literacy.

**Colin Sloper** is former director of the Centre for Professional Learning. He has been a teacher, assistant principal, and principal in government schools for the past thirty-five years. In the course of his career, he has been involved in the establishment of five new state government schools, spending the last seven years as principal at Pakenham Springs Primary School in Victoria. Because of his leadership and collaborative work with the school community, Pakenham Springs became the first recognized model of a PLC in Australia.

As a school leader, Colin has specialized in growing new schools by building a learning-focused culture throughout the school community. His leadership has emphasized student engagement while achieving substantial results for both the students and teachers he has served. Colin's schools are highly sought after as sites of professional learning for staff across all education sectors.

**Janelle Wills, PhD,** is the lead training associate for High Reliability Schools, The Art & Science of Teaching and other Marzano topics.

Personally trained by Robert J. Marzano, Dr. Wills specializes in long-term school improvement efforts. With over thirty years of teaching and leadership experience across all sectors of schooling, she has a strong commitment to continued learning that enables her to remain both informed and innovative in her approach. In her previous role as director of teaching and learning at Independent Schools Queensland, Dr. Wills was responsible for leading a team of accomplished professionals with specialist knowledge across a range of areas.

Dr. Wills holds a PhD in education. Her thesis focused on self-efficacy and contributed to multiple fields of knowledge, including special education, gifted education, assessment, and feedback.

# FOREWORD
## By Alma Harris and Michelle Jones

The idea of a professional learning community (PLC) has become commonplace in the international research and professional learning literature. Under the right conditions, a PLC can be a powerful staff development approach and a potent strategy for school transformation and change.

Empirical evidence suggests that improvement in student achievement through PLCs is accomplished as leaders and teachers collaboratively focus on securing quality learning for all students. In short, professional learning communities have three core purposes: (1) professional learning, (2) changes in instructional practice, and (3) collective capacity building.

Increasingly, evidence shows that teacher collaboration, in the form of collaborative teams, leads to increased teacher efficacy and better classroom performance. Furthermore, this evidence proposes that teachers working in a PLC can be a force for positive change and that, collectively, they can provide a powerful platform for educational transformation.

While there is a large corpus of literature on the subject of professional learning communities, the field is missing a contemporary, grounded, practical resource that explores the relationship between PLCs and transformational practice. *Transformative Collaboration* is such a book. It brings together practical wisdom and a clear theory of action. The five commitments for leading a PLC underscore the importance of clarity, trust, and evidence-informed action. The book is a tour de force of illustration, explanation, and exploration of effective PLCs in action.

*Transformative Collaboration* is a book that offers an alternative perspective on PLCs, one that is predicated on deep professional trust and genuine professional autonomy. This book is not just about PLCs; it addresses the way in which professional collaboration can be a mechanism for positive school and system level transformation and change.

*Transformative Collaboration* offers leaders and teachers around the globe a concrete and research-based reason to work collectively and collaboratively. In the face of a global reform process increasingly predicated on standardization, conformity, and de-professionalism, this book will reinforce why teachers must be at the heart of collaborative change processes, not simply as recipients, but as the drivers and architects of school transformation and improvement.

# INTRODUCTION

You would be hard pressed to find a team, school, or system in education today that is not working to become more effective. From Robert J. Marzano and Michael Fullan to Dylan Wiliam, Michelle Jones, and Alma Harris, there is consensus among the world's leading education researchers that a collaborative approach to practice is the best way for schools to achieve results and improve student learning.

The authors of this book have cumulatively supported over one thousand schools in Australia and New Zealand to cultivate the collaborative culture required to meet the academic and social needs of every student. *Transformative Collaboration: Five Commitments for Leading a Professional Learning Community* is the outcome of this experience, in combination with research from the field and educators' own views on how schools can make collaboration a priority. It is a book that takes you beneath the surface of the school as PLC to explore the critical commitments that leaders must make in order to truly transform school culture and get the results that students deserve.

## WHAT IS TRANSFORMATIVE COLLABORATION?

*Collaboration* is when colleagues in a school come together to share ideas, tools, and strategies in order to make key curriculum, assessment, instruction, teacher development, and leadership decisions. *Transformative collaboration* refers to the way in which PLCs use collaborative practice as the key lever for cultural and structural change that directly improves student and teacher learning.

Based on our experiences in schools, we strongly believe that collaboration is the key to transforming schools. In an education setting, transformation through collaboration is likely to involve changes in beliefs, structures, attitudes, and perceptions on schooling. In this respect, a PLC has the following transformative goals.

- Ensure that all students can and will learn at high levels.
- Create conditions that enable teachers to work collaboratively to improve learning.

- Monitor through data the impact of the school's actions on student learning success.

- Recognize people as the school's greatest resource and provide a corresponding level of professional learning and support.

- Ensure that the structures and culture of the school are inherently learning centered.

- Do things not because they are easy, convenient, or conventional but because they are right for students.

- Rigorously investigate approaches and strategies for increasing the professional dialogue on which student learning depends.

# HOW TO USE THIS BOOK

*Transformative Collaboration* provides insights, tips, and techniques to help you transform your school through collaboration with the goal of becoming a high-performing PLC. Each chapter revolves around one of the five commitments for leading a PLC that we have identified through experience and research as essential to the transformation process. Each chapter of the book contains the following elements.

- **KEY ACTIONS:** Within each commitment, we propose three key actions that leaders must take if their goal is wide-ranging, long-lasting school improvement that supports all students in learning at high levels. As well as explaining the research that underpins the identified actions, each chapter contains scenarios drawn from our work with schools in order to demonstrate what the PLC transformation looks like in a real-world context.

- **REFLECTION:** In this section, we reiterate the main points of the chapter and explain what leaders must do to put what they have learned into practice. In each chapter, we also provide reflective questions for each of the key actions discussed in the chapter, which leaders can use to track the progress of their school's transformation into a PLC.

- **INSIGHTS FROM THE FIELD:** Each chapter concludes with stories from PLC leaders, told in their own words, that shed further light or provide food for thought in relation to the commitment being discussed.

The checklist in figure I.1 lists each of the five commitments and related actions that are essential for transformative collaboration.

## COMMITMENT 1: UNDERSTAND WHAT IT MEANS TO BE A PLC

| | HAVEN'T CONSIDERED IT | THINKING ABOUT IT | IMPLEMENTING IT |
|---|---|---|---|
| **ACTION 1.1:** Understand the purpose of a PLC. | | | |
| **ACTION 1.2:** Understand the PLC process. | | | |
| **ACTION 1.3:** Understand professional learning within the PLC context. | | | |
| **COMMENTS** | | | |

## COMMITMENT 2: FIND THE COURAGE YOU NEED TO LEAD

| | HAVEN'T CONSIDERED IT | THINKING ABOUT IT | IMPLEMENTING IT |
|---|---|---|---|
| **ACTION 2.1:** Find the courage to challenge convention. | | | |
| **ACTION 2.2:** Find the courage to commit to growth. | | | |
| **ACTION 2.3:** Find the courage to focus on what works. | | | |
| **COMMENTS** | | | |

## COMMITMENT 3: BUILD A CLIMATE OF TRUST

| | HAVEN'T CONSIDERED IT | THINKING ABOUT IT | IMPLEMENTING IT |
|---|---|---|---|
| **ACTION 3.1:** Build behaviors that promote trust. | | | |
| **ACTION 3.2:** Build bridges to repair trust. | | | |
| **ACTION 3.3:** Build authenticity in your Interactions. | | | |
| **COMMENTS** | | | |

**Figure I.1:** Checklist of commitments and key actions.

*continued* →

## COMMITMENT 4: SHAPE SCHOOL STRUCTURES FOR SUCCESS

| | HAVEN'T CONSIDERED IT | THINKING ABOUT IT | IMPLEMENTING IT |
|---|---|---|---|
| **ACTION 4.1:** Connect structures and culture. | | | |
| **ACTION 4.2:** Change structures through school leadership. | | | |
| **ACTION 4.3:** Cultivate structures for a high-performing PLC. | | | |
| **COMMENTS** | | | |

## COMMITMENT 5: CREATE CLARITY IN COLLABORATION

| | HAVEN'T CONSIDERED IT | THINKING ABOUT IT | IMPLEMENTING IT |
|---|---|---|---|
| **ACTION 5.1:** Create clarity for shared understanding. | | | |
| **ACTION 5.2:** Create clarity of purpose, process, and product. | | | |
| **ACTION 5.3:** Create clarity with protocols. | | | |
| **COMMENTS** | | | |

# CHAPTER 1
# Understand What It Means to Be a PLC

*A professional learning community is a group of connected and engaged professionals who are responsible for driving change and improvement within, between and across schools that will directly benefit learners.*

—Alma Harris and Michelle Jones

As more and more PLCs are established within schools, the first priority of school leaders is to develop an understanding of why and how this approach provides the best results when it comes to whole-school improvement. In striving to build an understanding of the process and purpose of a PLC, schools can take the first of many steps on the PLC journey toward achieving high levels of learning for all students.

## KEY ACTIONS

Three key actions are essential to understand commitment 1, what it means to be a PLC.

- **ACTION 1.1:** Understand the purpose of a PLC.
- **ACTION 1.2:** Understand the PLC process.
- **ACTION 1.3:** Understand where professional learning sits within the PLC context.

### ACTION 1.1: UNDERSTAND THE PURPOSE OF A PLC

*Why?* This simple but powerful question sits at the heart of courageous PLC leadership. Simon Sinek (2009), who is internationally renowned for his work on leadership, shared the following insight during a popular TED Talk:

> Every single person, every single organization on the planet knows what they do, 100 percent. Some know how they do it. . . . But very, very few people or organizations know why they do what they do. By "why," I mean: What's your purpose? What's your cause? What's your belief? Why does your organization exist? Why do you get out of bed in the morning? And why should anyone care?

Unfortunately, many educators continue to operate in school communities that lack a sense of purpose in relation to student learning. School leaders can become so preoccupied by bureaucratic and accountability concerns that they never quite find the time to contemplate—let alone commit to—what their school's mission and vision might be in relation to the students it supposedly serves. The problem with this lack of direction is vividly portrayed by Lewis Carroll (1865) in *Alice's Adventures in Wonderland* when Alice encounters the Cheshire Cat at a fork in the road and seeks his advice about which route to take:

> "Would you tell me, please, which way I ought to go from here?"
>
> "That depends a good deal on where you want to get to," said the Cat.
>
> "I don't much care where—" said Alice.
>
> "Then it doesn't matter which way you go," said the Cat.

The point is that until Alice decides on the purpose of her journey, she cannot know which road will take her in the direction she wants to go. There are many schools today that function like Alice in this moment: caught at the fork in the road, they are suspended in a holding pattern, too tentative or too distracted to make a commitment to change. Without the sense of purpose required to make informed decisions, these conventional schools often end up choosing the road dictated by external stakeholders, system leaders, and policymakers. As a result, they remain teacher centric, curriculum centric, and compliance centric to the point of inertia. While school leaders and teachers struggle to meet the never-ending challenges that external education authorities mete out, students—supposedly the heart and soul of the school system—are all but forgotten.

In contrast to the directionlessness that often characterizes conventional schools, every PLC shares the same foundational purpose: *high levels of learning for all students*. In this way, PLCs place student learning at the center of both the day-to-day operations of the school and its larger vision for transformative collaboration. What's more, unlike the top-down approach to improvement common in conventional schools, in a PLC, all participants in the school community have a role to play in making high levels of learning a reality for all students.

- **SCHOOL LEADERS** need to understand how to engineer supportive conditions so that teachers and students can focus on the core business of learning.
- **TEACHERS** need to understand how to engage in the collaborative enterprise of monitoring and improving curriculum, assessment, and instruction to support student learning.
- **STUDENTS** need to understand implicitly that their school will not fail them.
- **PARENTS** need to understand that the school is constantly reviewing practices and structures to ensure that all students will be successful learners.

Only when there is communitywide agreement about the fundamental purpose of a PLC—high levels of learning for all students—can there be a clear direction and agreed-on practices that build collective capacity and collective action. As a result, the leader who commits to this clear purpose, communicates it to staff members, connects it to concrete actions, and personifies it through everyday leadership behaviors is already a step ahead on the road to transformative collaboration.

## ACTION 1.2: UNDERSTAND THE PLC PROCESS

PLCs advocate migrating away from a traditionally independent, isolated, individualist paradigm toward a truly collaborative and integrated organization with student learning at its heart. But how can school achieve this goal? What does the process look like, and what can schools expect? If you are a school leader starting the journey of transforming your organization into a PLC, the following priorities are imperative when it comes to building the capacity for transformation.

- Create a schoolwide culture.
- Establish effective collaborative teams.
- Use evidence to improve teaching and learning.

### CREATE A SCHOOLWIDE CULTURE

School culture has been defined as "the deeper level of basic assumptions and beliefs that are shared by members of an organization, that operate unconsciously, and that define in a basic 'take-for-granted' fashion an organization's view of itself and its environment" (Schein, 1985, p. 6). A school's culture is the lens through which others view and evaluate the daily work of educators. Simply put, school culture is the *way we do things around here*.

School culture has been one of the most neglected aspects of the school improvement process. For decades, it has been written off as the exclusive domain of the school leader or leadership team, whose sole responsibility it is to create the culture necessary to drive improvement. When this occurs, an unhealthy mindset of isolation and dependency starts to infiltrate the school. Teachers begin to perceive themselves as followers rather than leaders of learning, and this perpetuates a culture of maintaining the status quo and discourages meaningful change.

In contrast, PLCs put culture at the heart of continuous improvement so that it becomes the platform that anchors educational innovation. PLC leaders emphasize innovation and renewal by prioritizing interactions that build high levels of professional trust and collective capacity in order to have an impact on teacher practice and student achievement. As PLC experts Richard DuFour and Mike Mattos (2013) recognize, the most powerful way to improve both teaching and learning "is not by micromanaging instruction but by creating the collaborative culture and collective responsibility of a professional learning community." As the collective understanding of PLCs matures within a school, the school continually sharpens its focus on learning to improve student achievement.

Richard DuFour, Rebecca DuFour, Robert Eaker, Thomas W. Many, and Mike Mattos (2016) recognize the importance of school culture in their foundational PLC handbook *Learning by Doing*. DuFour and his coauthors (2016) state that a school aiming to transform into a PLC should look to make the following shifts:

- From independence . . . to interdependence
- From a language of complaint . . . to a language of commitment
- From long-term strategic planning . . . to planning for short-term wins
- From infrequent generic recognition . . . to frequent specific recognition and a culture of celebration that creates many winners (p. 259)

These elements serve as useful markers in a PLC leader's efforts to monitor the evolution of the school's collaborative culture.

## ESTABLISH EFFECTIVE COLLABORATIVE TEAMS

A key tenet of PLCs is the establishment of collaborative teams (DuFour et al., 2016). Educators within a PLC form smaller collaborative teams, which then meet on a regular basis to share knowledge, analyze data, and generate new ways of functioning in order to best support the learning of the students they serve. Collaborative teams "may be various sizes, include members with similar or different roles or responsibilities, and meet frequently face-to-face, virtually, or through a combination" (Learning Forward, 2015), but they are always guided by the premise that only through sustained collaborative work can schools achieve their mission of high levels of learning for all.

In conventional schools, teacher teams have traditionally operated based on a combination of two styles of interpersonal engagement: (1) *coordination* and (2) *collegiality*. To coordinate as a team is to organize diverse elements together in a congruous operation. Teacher teams coordinate in school communities to achieve valuable goals, just as organizers would to stage a sporting event or arts festival. When coordination is the dominant approach, all teachers have allocated and specific roles that they perform in isolation but that contribute to the success of the school.

As an example, consider the following scenario highlighting a coordination approach.

> A grade-level collaborative team is meeting to devise a new set of assessment tasks. There are five teachers on the team, and each teacher designs one question to contribute to the formative assessment task. Because this team tends toward a coordination-based engagement style, the teachers design their contributions in isolation, and then they collect and combine the five discrete assessment activities into one long assessment task. They have completed the task, but there is only a minimum of common understanding as to the learning targets, criteria, and marking rubric.

The collegial style of engagement prioritizes strong professional relationships among fellow educators. Collegiality is conducive to a friendly and respectful environment that promotes goodwill among colleagues. However, it can also be counterproductive, as in this scenario.

> A grade-level collaborative team is meeting to devise a new set of assessment tasks. Vanesh, an experienced teacher, presents a task from the previous year's assessment without any adjustments. The task does not relate to the new learning targets or success criteria. The other members of the team recognize it as one of Vanesh's recycled favorite tasks, which he has included many times previously because it is quick to mark and keeps the students busy. The other team members accept Vanesh's assessment task despite its lack of relevance because they do not want to jeopardize their personal and professional relationships with him and the other members of the team.

Needless to say, there will be many times when teachers still need to coordinate and act collegially in order to successfully provide the services required of them. In a conventional school, however, these forms of interaction may perpetuate isolated, solution-driven professional practices that offer the promise of a quick fix but cannot provide sustained solutions. In contrast, PLCs explicitly focus on creating the conditions for positive collective inquiry through *collaboration*: an intentional way of interacting with the aim of improving professional practice in order to achieve and sustain better outcomes for learners. DuFour et al. (2016) explain:

> In a PLC, collaboration represents a systematic process in which teachers work together interdependently in order to impact their classroom practice in ways that will lead to better results for their students, for their team, and for their school. (p. 12)

The practice of collaboration dictates that to have a transformative impact on learning, education professionals need to work together in new ways, using new skills and new understandings to move beyond coordination and collegiality into the collaborative construction of new learning. The following scenario shows how this might look.

> A grade-level collaborative team is meeting to devise a new set of assessment tasks. Because the school has recently embarked on the journey toward becoming a PLC, the teachers in the team are aware of how important it is to gather useful formative data about what students are learning. They begin their task by collectively revisiting the curriculum in order to refresh their understanding of the knowledge and skills that their students need to learn. They identify the key learning goals that the assessment tasks will measure and work together to create a set of integrated tasks based on the learning goals. At their next meeting, a week later, the teachers set aside time to revisit their assessment tasks and establish a common rubric that they will each use to guide the grading process. When the team collates the data from each team member, it is able to establish clear areas of strength and weakness that it can use for future collaborative planning.

Collaborative teams that set realistic, evidence-based learning goals and work continually to improve student learning become the living embodiment of the school improvement plan (DuFour & Fullan, 2013). In order to make this transformation a reality, however, teams must attend to a third aspect of the PLC process: using evidence to improve teaching and learning.

## USE EVIDENCE TO IMPROVE TEACHING AND LEARNING

To transform an existing teacher team into a high-functioning collaborative team, the team must begin the powerful process of using evidence to improve learning. According to professor and researcher Stephen Dinham (2008), "Professional learning needs to be built upon an evidential foundation of what works in teaching, not fad, fantasy, idealism, ideology or rhetoric." The evidence collaborative teams collect on an ongoing basis provides the impetus for teachers to inquire into best practice. This evidence centers on student learning achievement without exception.

In schools where PLCs thrive, teams adopt a results-orientated approach to achieve their purpose of ensuring high levels of learning for all students. Consequently, collaborative team meetings in a PLC routinely involve discussion of questions such as those recommended by Harris and Jones (2012) in a National College for School Leadership resource on collaboration in professional learning, which is central to a PLC:

- What is the evidence telling us about the new strategies we are using?
- Does the feedback require that we make some adjustment or refinement to the strategies?

- Does the feedback fit what we anticipated or what we already know, or are there some challenges to our thinking?

- Are we able to agree on a shared and clear view of what the trial is telling us?

- Can we agree on a way forward? (p. 20)

Ultimately, if data indicate that the team's collaboration efforts have not resulted in improved outcomes for students, then the team has to question whether it was focused on the right instruction, assessment, or intervention to begin with. The following scenario illustrates how this situation might play out in a PLC.

Lena, the experienced deputy principal of a large secondary school, has long been the school's designated point of contact for external standardized assessments. Each year, she ensures that the standardized assessments are administered correctly to each cohort, and then she waits to receive the final results of state and national tests. Within her annual schedule, she assigns blocks of undisturbed time to meticulously unpack and analyze the data. The analysis is a lengthy process, but Lena takes pleasure in it because mathematics is her specialist teaching area. She prioritizes this responsibility and feels highly accountable in her role as interpreter of the data for the school community.

Once she has scrutinized the standardized assessment data, Lena calls a meeting of department heads to inform them about the academic trends revealed by the data and share her professional insights. The department heads then return to their departmental teams and communicate the data trends to their teaching staff. Teachers identify students who have scored below the minimum standard and assign them to a remediation group for the next semester, where they monitor them every term for improvement.

Lena has been disseminating data in this manner for many years. She believes her method to be quick and efficient, and it meets her accountability requirements at a system level. Heads of department are appreciative of Lena's expertise in data literacy, as they feel that they lack the skills to interpret the data accurately.

As time goes by, this culture of data dissemination—in which information passes from Lena to the heads of department and then from department heads to the teaching staff—becomes deeply embedded in the school. At the same time, however, it becomes increasingly apparent that despite Lena's hard work and dedication, the students' results show no improvement. In fact, student performance is noticeably declining in certain learning areas, including Lena's own mathematics department. What's more, the students

*continued →*

identified to receive remediation are the same students year after year, in what appears to be an eternal cycle of intervention.

Anxious about how to turn this predicament around, the school's leadership team begins to investigate the possibility of developing a set of questions designed to support each collaborative team to analyze its own formative and summative assessment data. Many staff members are hesitant, but two departmental teams agree to trial the set of data questions, which include inquiry into assessment design, delivery, and relevance.

The teams agree to focus on sharing wisdom rather than making judgments about the data. As they become more confident in using the questions, they begin to share insights about the data with their colleagues in other departments. Over time, they build on their understanding of the data by swapping teaching strategies and ideas about instruction, differentiation, and formative assessment practices. When members of one team start to observe one another's instruction in the classroom environment, a few other departments recognize this as a good idea and also begin to observe each other's practice in their area of instruction.

Although the new method is a success when it comes to fostering collaboration among teachers, it soon becomes apparent that professional learning is required to improve data literacy skills across the middle-management team. To deal with this issue, Lena asks two other teachers of mathematics to co-facilitate a series of professional learning sessions to help staff refine their skills in this area. The sessions are well attended, and teachers express a sense of increased confidence in discussing student progress because they now share a common understanding of the evidence. Meanwhile, as departments begin to spend more common planning time unwrapping student data, they start to generate some simple but manageable forms of intervention targeted at the specific needs of these students, maximizing the additional time and support they receive.

Lena initially finds it extremely challenging to release the school's data to other teachers. As she observes the progress of the collaborative teams, however, she is excited to see the difference it makes in terms of the conversations she hears about learning. Increasingly, she notices that the teachers are discussing student learning growth with a heightened sense of positivity and encouragement. As Lena no longer has to invest significant time to analyze whole-school data, she chooses to use that time to visit departmental team meetings. To keep her finger on the data pulse, she attends at least one meeting every two weeks and engages in data conversations with that team. It does not take long before student achievement begins noticeably to increase.

This scenario is typical of many teams. It demonstrates that increasing data literacy through collaboration is a high-leverage practice that improves the integrity of the assessment design process, the quality of teacher feedback, the efficiency of student-data analysis, and, ultimately, student results.

## ACTION 1.3: UNDERSTAND PROFESSIONAL LEARNING WITHIN THE PLC CONTEXT

A growing body of education research indicates that the most effective teacher learning activities—those that have the biggest impact on student achievement—involve forms of job-embedded professional learning (Coggshall, Rasmussen, Colton, Milton, & Jacques, 2012). Educators throughout the world are quickly recognizing that establishing and developing effective professional learning is their best hope for sustained improvement in student outcomes. Collaborating on areas critical to teacher development is becoming more commonplace.

While there is nothing new about teachers working together, there is a new understanding about the conditions necessary to support this collective engagement. Specifically, there is a visible shift in educational best practice from professional development, in which teachers are positioned as the passive recipients of predetermined knowledge or skills, to professional learning, which requires that teachers take an active role in the co-construction of professional knowledge. In a paper for the Australian Institute for Teaching and School Leadership, Diane Mayer and Margaret Lloyd (2011) make a point of noting this distinction:

> One issue that needs clarification at the outset is the use of the terms professional development and professional learning. . . . Various authors have, for some time now, been critical of professional development conceived of as something that one "does," or that is "provided," or is "done to" teachers, and that has promoted the notion that it must be closely tied to the context of teaching and the capacities of teachers. . . . The shift in terminology away from professional development . . . may well reside in these perceptions and the presumed "baggage" associated with poorly conceived, fragmented, one-shot and de-contextualised "in-service workshops." (p. 3)

This perspective is supported by Canadian education researcher Michael Fullan (2007), who writes in no uncertain terms that "we must abandon professional development and make professional learning an everyday experience for all educators" (p. 36). Professional development is being subsumed by the more cohesive and dynamic approach that Is professional learning.

It is well-established that the conventional approach of professional development rarely leads to schoolwide change. In contrast, the PLC approach of professional learning reveals the way in which collective capacity can be harnessed to improve teacher quality throughout the entire school community. Professional learning in a PLC becomes a shared enterprise that is generated by and belongs to the whole school community. Although school leaders remain necessary to coordinate professional learning and maintain enthusiasm for the work, they must also relinquish some control over the process by inviting all members of the community to assume mutual responsibility for ongoing school-based inquiry. The primary aim for leaders of effective PLCs should be to empower other professionals to learn (DuFour et al., 2016). For this reason, as Fullan (2011) remarks, professional learning in a PLC is a never-ending journey of continuous improvement.

# REFLECTION

The key message in this chapter is that it takes informed, knowledgeable leadership to effect the changes required to become a PLC. To lead a successful PLC, a leader must grasp the purpose and process of becoming a PLC as well as the role of professional learning. An effective PLC leader has a deep yet ever-evolving understanding of what it means to be a PLC and is able to leverage this knowledge to engineer the conditions for transformation to occur.

For leaders seeking to develop their understanding of what it means to be a PLC, it may help to think of leading the PLC process as analogous to an orb-weaver spider spinning its web. The spider must sense a change in vibration before successfully reeling the first strand, then the spider immediately strengthens this initial strand with several strong radials and continually fortifies it with circular threads. Similarly, leaders who embark on the PLC process do so because they are responding to identifiable gaps in student achievement. The center of the web is fused together by data, and all PLC actions and interactions radiate as a direct response to that data. Once the first elements of the PLC are in place, the leader fortifies them by providing the school culture and structures necessary for success.

# REFLECTIVE QUESTIONS: COMMITMENT 1— UNDERSTAND WHAT IT MEANS TO BE A PLC

As you consider each reflective question, contemplate your response and identify the evidence that supports your thinking.

## ACTION 1.1: UNDERSTAND THE PURPOSE OF A PLC

- How might you explain what you do to ensure high levels of learning for all students at your school?
- What are your beliefs on how student learning can become a central focus in your leadership?

## ACTION 1.2: UNDERSTAND THE PLC PROCESS

- What does a high-functioning PLC look like, feel like, and sound like?
- How can you create the necessary conditions for teachers to analyze data, plan instruction, and adjust practices collaboratively?

## ACTION 1.3: UNDERSTAND PROFESSIONAL LEARNING WITHIN THE PLC CONTEXT

- What steps can you take to ensure professional learning is job embedded in your school?
- In what ways might the collaborative teams lead the next phase of professional learning in your school?
- How will you broker the resources and support for job-embedded professional learning to thrive?

# INSIGHTS FROM THE FIELD

*I reckon the PLC process just flows on from team teaching. I always like to work with people and share ideas, and the PLC is just building on that but making it more formal so that it's something you actually follow. I think collaboration arises from the way the teams are selected to work together, so that they've got different skills. It's best to have people in a team with a variety of different skills and different talents, not only to share the responsibility but to see things from a different perspective. That we trust one another is the thing.*

*Working in a PLC has made the academic side of things more stringent. We have our essential standards, and all our planning comes directly from that. Before we would come in and go, "I want something pretty to put up on the wall," but now we make sure the kids are aware of the reason that we're asking them to complete these tasks.*

*I am really in tune to what the kids do know and what they don't know. It used to be that when we'd taught something, we'd taught it, and if the kids weren't listening then bad luck—but now we're really encouraging the children to have more ownership of their learning. Doing it as a whole school, everyone's on the same wavelength.*

—JESSICA, SIXTH-GRADE TEACHER

*In our PLC, we want student learning to be an ongoing developmental learning process that everybody has ownership of. One of the things that was important to us from the very early days was that it couldn't be a top-down process and we needed everybody to be involved. By asking people to contribute and talk about what it is they did or didn't understand, we keep the lines of communication open. The ownership had to come back to all of us. I think that's really important.*

*Ultimately, it really isn't about the teaching. It really has become more about the learning. We say, "They haven't got it; I need to do something—we need to do something so that these kids have learned it." We used to say, "This is the way I'm going to do it, and bad luck if you don't get it," but now it's a case of, "Well, they didn't get it this way, so what other ways can I do it?" Teachers can try different methods and then compare the results they've got with results from other teachers. I think the power to become a better teacher is driven by the data and driven by the collaborative team approach as well.*

—IVY, ASSISTANT PRINCIPAL

*We had a lot of discussions early on about the culture of the school. What was the background of the clientele coming to the school? What were teachers observing in their classrooms? What was the best way to move kids forward? Where were the best opportunities for kids? Every answer to these questions came back to learning. Learning was a pathway through poverty and disadvantage. It was a fairly big impetus for staff that if we wanted to help these kids, it wouldn't be the fluffy stuff that we needed to do. We needed to do the core learning stuff, because that's actually their way out of poverty.*

*Our kids give feedback to the teachers now. They point out when the learning goals aren't actually learning focused.*

—CHRIS, PRINCIPAL

*The PLC transformation has been a steep learning curve. In the past, our whole focus was redoing the school and a lot of building stuff. That was more of a focus than curriculum and student learning, which was often just ad hoc. The PLC process has definitely rejuvenated me as a principal in that I now understand where we're going, what we're trying to do, and why we're trying to do it. I've got a greater purpose as an educational leader. I'm more involved in student learning than I was previously.*

*I enjoy seeing that we're heading in the right direction, and I enjoy the fact that I think most staff are pretty committed to it. I think staff members who leave here now and apply for a job anywhere else are going to be much better prepared because they can actually talk about how you improve student learning. It gives you the* how *rather than "I'll do this, and it might help," so I think they're better placed.*

—DREW, PRINCIPAL

# CHAPTER 2

# Find the Courage You Need to Lead

*The courage to lead is forged when something personally meaningful is at stake for you and for those in your sphere of influence. The vision must really matter to you. . . . Courageous leadership action comes from your commitment to your deeply held beliefs about the issue.*

—Timothy D. Kanold

In reference to urban education, business professor and theorist Jeffrey Pfeffer (2007) describes improving student achievement as a hill to be climbed:

> People have built quite successful careers—describing the hill, measuring the hill, walking around the hill, taking pictures of the hill, and so forth. Sooner or later, somebody needs to actually climb the hill. (p. 137)

In our view, leading a PLC is also much like a hill to climb—although given the challenges involved, some may maintain that PLC leadership would be better termed a *mountain* to climb. Indeed, the following are just some of the difficulties that leaders face when it comes to transforming a school into a PLC.

- Releasing ownership over collective inquiry to all the members of the learning community and resisting the temptation to take control of the process
- Promoting mutual responsibility for moving the inquiry process forward and resisting the temptation to provide solutions
- Embracing conflict as a way to solve problems while resisting the temptation to advocate personal preferences
- Articulating and modeling a clear understanding of collaborative inquiry and resisting the temptation to revert to quick fixes
- Leading a learning culture and resisting the temptation to leave learning-centered leadership to others

Just like climbing a mountain, the notion of transforming a school into a high-performing PLC can seem daunting and overwhelming. Many questions abound: Where do I begin? Where is the correct path? How long will it take? What if I fail or get lost? Like mountain-climbing, the commitment to lead a PLC requires the strong belief that the effort is worth it—that the summit will unveil new vistas, and that schools will reap rewards when they reach their ultimate goal.

Commitment 2 in the PLC transformation incorporates the ideas of several thought leaders within the field of leadership. In particular, it draws on the work of Robert J. Marzano, whose highly acclaimed life's work has been dedicated to the study of effective teaching and leadership. Marzano has concluded that the best environment for great teaching and leadership is a powerful PLC (DuFour & Marzano, 2011), and he provides compelling evidence that can help to guide leaders through the important journey of school transformation.

# KEY ACTIONS

To explain commitment 2, we will outline three key actions.

- **ACTION 2.1:** Find the courage to challenge convention.
- **ACTION 2.2:** Find the courage to commit to growth.
- **ACTION 2.3:** Find the courage to focus on what works.

## ACTION 2.1: FIND THE COURAGE TO CHALLENGE CONVENTION

It is an incontestable fact that quality of education directly impacts an individual's chances later in life. Education researcher John Hattie (2012) calculates that high school graduates earn 48 percent more than those who do not complete high school; they also live six to nine years longer and are 10 to 20 percent less likely to be involved in criminal activity. What's more, it isn't just a matter of simply attending school, since research has shown that "whether a school operates effectively or not increases or decreases a student's chances of academic success" (Marzano, Waters, & McNulty, 2005, p. 3). From their meta-analysis of thirty-five years of research, Robert J. Marzano, Timothy Waters, and Brian A. McNulty (2005) conclude that "school leadership has a substantial effect on student achievement" (p. 12), while earlier research indicates that in higher-gain schools, teachers report their school leaders to be more active participants in teacher learning than in lower-gain schools (Bamburg & Andrews, 1991).

Few leaders would argue with the statement that schools should provide high levels of learning for every student, and most would be quick to affirm the idea that their own work makes this possible. But how often do their thoughts, words, and actions align with this belief? Our own experiences suggest that walking the talk of PLC leadership may be easier said than done. When presenting to fellow educators, we have on many occasions put forward the foundational PLC belief that all students can learn, only to be met by an audience member's incredulous questions: "Do you mean *all* students? Surely you don't mean *all* students . . . ? Don't you believe in differentiation? We can't have high expectations for every student."

Although these skeptical educators would likely concede that every student *should* learn, the conventional discourse that they have internalized means that they simply do not believe that all students *can* learn at high levels—even though research Indicates that the PLC approach to school improvement can measurably improve learning outcomes for every student without exception (Marzano, Heflebower, Hoegh, Warrick, & Grift, 2016). Entrenched attitudes of this type are often unconscious, but they can have a chilling effect on a school's ability to create meaningful, lasting change.

As this example demonstrates, to implement research-based initiatives that will transform schools requires a powerful commitment to change the status quo (Marzano, 2003). Whereas conventional schools resist anything that may lead to institutional change, the collective inquiry process in a PLC is motivated by the belief that it is possible to transform collaboration, curriculum, assessment, instruction, and teacher development in ways that will ensure high levels of learning for all students. And while leaders in a conventional school assume what psychologist Carol Dweck (2006) terms a *fixed mindset*, upholding the status quo by perpetuating time-honored traditions and behaviors irrespective of their impact on student learning outcomes, PLC leaders have a *growth mindset* that enables them to intentionally disrupt the status quo in order to ask the right questions and generate innovative responses.

If the goal of the PLC process is to make certain that all students have access to the advantages that a high-quality education confers, school leaders must do everything they can to ensure that their school provides high levels of learning for every student. As the acclaimed Harvard researcher Ronald Edmonds (1979) reminds us in his three declarative statements:

> (a) We can, whenever and wherever we choose, successfully teach all children whose schooling is of interest to us; (b) We already know more than we need to do that; and (c) Whether or not we do it must finally depend on how we feel about the fact that we haven't so far. (p. 23)

## ACTION 2.2: FIND THE COURAGE TO COMMIT TO GROWTH

When PLC leaders find the courage to challenge the status quo, they move from a laissez-faire approach to school improvement to one that leaves no convention unexamined (Kanold, 2011). In doing so, they begin to ask the kind of questions that could have far-reaching implications for the culture and structures of the school:

> What school characteristics and practices have been most successful in helping all students achieve at high levels? How could we adopt those characteristics and practices in our own school? What commitments would we have to make to one another to create such a school? What indicators could we monitor to assess our progress? (DuFour, 2004)

To answer these questions, PLC leaders may turn to the vast and ever-expanding body of research that exists on effective leadership. Robert J. Marzano, Phil Warrick, and Julia A.

Simms (2014) synthesize much of this research in *A Handbook for High Reliability Schools*. Marzano and his colleagues (2014) provide a persuasive, evidence-based picture of what highly effective schools do to increase achievement for each and every student. Table 2.1 organizes key elements cited throughout the research literature as essential for improving learning outcomes for all students as a framework of five hierarchical levels.

**Table 2.1:** The Five Levels of Operation for a High Reliability School and Related Critical Commitments

| LEVEL 5<br>COMPETENCY-BASED EDUCATION | Get rid of time requirements.<br>Adjust reporting systems accordingly. |
|---|---|
| LEVEL 4<br>STANDARDS-REFERENCED REPORTING | Develop proficiency scales for the essential content.<br>Report status and growth on the student report using proficiency scales. |
| LEVEL 3<br>GUARANTEED AND VIABLE CURRICULUM | Continually monitor the viability of the curriculum.<br>Create a comprehensive vocabulary program.<br>Use direct instruction for knowledge application and metacognitive skills. |
| LEVEL 2<br>EFFECTIVE TEACHING IN EVERY CLASSROOM | Create an evaluation system whose primary purpose is teacher development.<br>■ The system is comprehensive and specific.<br>■ The system includes a developmental scale.<br>■ The system acknowledges and supports growth. |
| LEVEL 1<br>SAFE AND COLLABORATIVE CULTURE | Implement the professional learning community process. |

*Source: Adapted from Marzano et al., 2014.*

The five levels outlined within the High Reliability Schools™ (HRS) framework enable schools to focus on sets of interlinked factors rather than isolated activities or initiatives. By grouping factors into the HRS levels, which represent increasing levels of sophistication, the factors become integrated acts of improvement targeted at increasing student achievement. The levels begin with those factors that cultivate professional collaboration and move through to those factors that address higher levels of learning for teachers and students within a culture of school improvement.

The critical commitment at level 1 of the framework is the development of a PLC. Level 1 is foundational to the HRS framework because the collaborative teams within a PLC provide the fertile conditions for the other HRS levels to flourish: "If students and faculty do not have a safe and collaborative culture in which to work, little if any substantive work can be accomplished" (Marzano et al., 2014, p. 4). As they work through the PLC process, collaborative teams will focus on improving instruction to ensure effective teaching in every classroom (level 2); develop a guaranteed and viable curriculum (level 3); and ultimately move toward standards-referenced reporting (level 4) and competency-based education (level 5).

It is important to note that schools typically approach levels 1, 2, and 3 simultaneously, even though level 1 sets the foundation. As teams systematically work on the critical commitments inherent within each level, their collaborative efforts become more focused and effective, since each step brings the school closer to its ultimate goal: high levels of learning for all.

## ACTION 2.3: FIND THE COURAGE TO FOCUS ON WHAT WORKS

The five-level HRS framework provides an indispensable overview of what PLC leaders need to do to effect transformation in their schools. However, it does not provide much insight into how educators should behave on a day-to-day basis. With so many competing demands for their attention, where should PLC leaders focus their energy to ensure that *high levels of learning for all* becomes not an empty slogan with no real meaning but a literal statement of guarantee?

In their meta-analysis that spans thirty-five years of research on school leadership, Marzano and his colleagues (2005) identify the twenty-one critical factors or responsibilities that most warrant attention by school leaders. The study also showed the general effects of school leadership, finding that the average correlation between leadership behavior and school achievement is 0.25—which means that an increase of one standard deviation in school leadership is associated with a ten-point gain in school achievement. The twenty-one responsibilities that the meta-analysis identifies, along with their correlation to student achievement, appear in table 2.2 (page 20).

A list of twenty-one responsibilities is certainly daunting. Immediately, questions of priority arise. Is each responsibility of equal importance? Are certain responsibilities worthy of more focused attention than others? Where is a leader's time and attention best spent?

As it happens, the amount of attention that each responsibility receives, and the approach taken, depends on the nature of the innovation or change being implemented (Marzano et al., 2005). Some innovations within schools require changes that are gradual and incremental— what Marzano and his colleagues (2005) call *first-order change*—while others require changes that are dramatic and sweeping, known as *second-order change*. Historically, when leadership techniques do not match the order of change required by an innovation, the innovation has failed irrespective of its merits (Marzano et al., 2005).

**Table 2.2:** The Twenty-One Responsibilities and Their Correlations (R) With Student Academic Achievement

| RESPONSIBILITIES | AVERAGE R | THE EXTENT TO WHICH THE PRINCIPAL . . . | ASSOCIATED PRACTICES |
|---|---|---|---|
| AFFIRMATION | 0.19 | Recognizes and celebrates accomplishments and acknowledges failures | ■ Systematically and fairly recognizes and celebrates accomplishments of teachers<br>■ Systematically and fairly recognizes and celebrates accomplishments of students<br>■ Systematically acknowledges failures and celebrates accomplishments of the school |
| CHANGE AGENT | 0.25 | Is willing to challenge and actively challenges the status quo | ■ Consciously challenges the status quo<br>■ Is comfortable with leading change initiatives with uncertain outcomes<br>■ Systematically considers new and better ways of doing things |
| COMMUNICATION | 0.23 | Establishes strong lines of communication with and among teachers and students | ■ Is easily accessible to teachers<br>■ Develops effective means for teachers to communicate with one another<br>■ Maintains open and effective lines of communication with staff |
| CONTINGENT REWARDS | 0.24 | Recognizes and rewards individual accomplishments | ■ Recognizes individuals who excel<br>■ Uses performance rather than seniority as the primary criterion for reward and advancement<br>■ Uses hard work and results as the basis for reward and recognition |
| CULTURE | 0.25 | Fosters shared beliefs and a sense of community and cooperation | ■ Promotes cooperation among staff<br>■ Promotes a sense of well-being<br>■ Promotes cohesion among staff<br>■ Develops an understanding of purpose<br>■ Develops a shared vision of what the school could be like |
| DISCIPLINE | 0.27 | Protects teachers from issues and influences that would detract from their teaching time or focus | ■ Protects instructional time from interruptions<br>■ Protects and shelters teachers from distractions |

| FLEXIBILITY | 0.28 | Adapts leadership behavior to the needs of the current situation and is comfortable with dissent | ■ Is comfortable with major changes in how things are done<br>■ Encourages people to express opinions even though these may differ from those in senior leadership roles<br>■ Adapts leadership style to needs of specific situations<br>■ Can adjust to be directive or nondirective as the situation requires |
|---|---|---|---|
| FOCUS | 0.24 | Establishes clear goals and keeps those goals in the forefront of the school's attention | ■ Establishes high, concrete goals and expectations that all students meet them<br>■ Establishes concrete goals for all curriculum, instruction, and assessment<br>■ Establishes concrete goals for the general functioning of the school<br>■ Continually keeps attention on established goals |
| IDEALS AND BELIEFS | 0.22 | Communicates and operates from strong ideals and beliefs about schooling | ■ Holds strong professional beliefs about schools, teaching, and learning<br>■ Shares beliefs about schooling, teaching, and learning with the staff<br>■ Demonstrates behaviors that are consistent with beliefs |
| INPUT | 0.25 | Involves teachers in the design and implementation of important decisions and policies | ■ Provides opportunity for input on all important decisions<br>■ Provides opportunities for staff to be involved in developing school policies<br>■ Uses leadership team in decision making |
| INTELLECTUAL STIMULATION | 0.24 | Ensures that staff are aware of the most current theories and practices and makes the discussion of these a regular aspect of the school's culture | ■ Keeps informed about current research and theory regarding effective schooling<br>■ Continually exposes the staff to contemporary ideas about how to be effective<br>■ Systematically engages staff in discussions about current research and theory<br>■ Continually involves the staff in reading articles and books about evidence-based practices |

continued →

| RESPONSIBILITIES | AVERAGE R | THE EXTENT TO WHICH THE PRINCIPAL . . . | ASSOCIATED PRACTICES |
|---|---|---|---|
| INVOLVEMENT IN CURRICULUM, INSTRUCTION, AND ASSESSMENT | 0.20 | Is directly involved in the design and implementation of curriculum, instruction, and assessment practices | ■ Is involved in helping teachers design curricular activities<br>■ Is involved with teachers to address instructional issues in their classrooms<br>■ Is involved with teachers to address assessment issues |
| KNOWLEDGE OF CURRICULUM, INSTRUCTION, AND ASSESSMENT | 0.25 | Is knowledgeable about current curriculum, instruction, and assessment practices | ■ Is knowledgeable about instructional practices<br>■ Is knowledgeable about assessment practices<br>■ Provides conceptual guidance for teachers regarding effective classroom practice |
| MONITORING AND EVALUATING | 0.27 | Monitors the effectiveness of school practices and their impact on student learning | ■ Monitors and evaluates the effectiveness of curriculum, instruction, and assessment |
| OPTIMIZER | 0.20 | Inspires and leads new and challenging innovations | ■ Inspires teachers to accomplish things that might seem beyond their grasp<br>■ Portrays a positive attitude about the ability of the staff to accomplish substantial things<br>■ Is a driving force behind major initiatives |
| ORDER | 0.25 | Establishes a set of standard operating procedures and routines | ■ Provides and enforces clear structure, rules, and procedures for students<br>■ Provides and enforces clear structures, rules, and procedures for staff<br>■ Establishes routines regarding the running of the school that staff understand and follow |
| OUTREACH | 0.27 | Is an advocate and spokesperson for the school to all stakeholders | ■ Ensures that the school is in compliance with national and state requirements<br>■ Advocates on behalf of the school in the community<br>■ Advocates for the school with parents<br>■ Ensures that stakeholders are aware of the school's accomplishments |

| | | | |
|---|---|---|---|
| RELATIONSHIPS | 0.18 | Demonstrates an awareness of the personal aspects of teachers and staff | ■ Remains aware of personal needs of teachers<br>■ Maintains personal relationships with teachers<br>■ Is informed about significant personal issues within the lives of staff members<br>■ Acknowledges significant events in the lives of staff members |
| RESOURCES | 0.25 | Provides teachers with materials and professional development necessary for the successful execution of their jobs | ■ Ensures that teachers have necessary materials and equipment<br>■ Ensures that teachers have necessary staff development opportunities that directly enhance their teaching |
| SITUATIONAL AWARENESS | 0.33 | Is aware of the details and undercurrents in the operations of the school and uses this information to address current and potential issues | ■ Is aware of informal groups and relationships among staff of the school<br>■ Is aware of issues in the school that have not surfaced but could create discord<br>■ Can predict what could go wrong from day to day |
| VISIBILITY | 0.20 | Has quality contact and interactions with teachers and students | ■ Makes systematic, frequent visits to classrooms<br>■ Maintains high visibility around the school<br>■ Has frequent contact with students |

*Source: Adapted from Marzano et al., 2005.*

According to Marzano and his colleagues (2005), the typical human response is to address almost all problems as if they require small, incremental steps. However, when problems are complex—like the pivotal PLC problem of how to guarantee high levels of learning for all students—a more radical approach is required. As Fullan (2001) explains, "The big problems of the day are complex, rife with paradoxes and dilemmas. For these problems, there are no once-and-for-all answers" (p. 73). These problems require change that warrants decisive, swift action, since "schools that go slow and do a little at a time" may "end up doing so little that they succeed only in upsetting everything without accruing the benefits of change" (Theodore Sizer, as cited in Fullan, 1993, p. 78).

So, which of the twenty-one responsibilities are appropriate when first-order change is required, and which are most appropriate for second-order change? All the responsibilities define the standard operating procedures in a school and typify first-order change. Second-order change, however, is most closely related to seven of the twenty-one responsibilities. They are as follows.

1. Change agent

2. Flexibility

3. Ideals and beliefs

4. Intellectual simulation

5. Knowledge of curriculum, instruction, and assessment

6. Monitoring and evaluating

7. Optimizer

Let us consider each of these seven responsibilities briefly in relation to the role of a PLC leader.

## CHANGE AGENT

In alignment with action 2.1, this responsibility refers to the extent to which a leader is willing to challenge the status quo and upset a school's equilibrium in order to drive transformation. The specific behaviors and characteristics associated with this responsibility are as follows:

- Consciously challenging the status quo

- Being willing to lead change initiatives with uncertain outcomes

- Systematically considering new and better ways of doing things

- Consistently attempting to operate at the edge versus the center of the school's competence (Marzano et al., 2005, p. 45)

In research involving interviews with nineteen principals, education leadership expert David Gurr (2002) finds that these leaders "generally describe themselves . . . as showing transformational leadership qualities" (p. 90). According to Bernard M. Bass and Bruce J. Avolio (1995), transformational leadership is:

> a process in which the leaders take actions to increase their associates' awareness of what is right and important, to raise their associates' motivational maturity and to move their associates to go beyond the associates' own self-interests for the good of the group, organization, or society. (p. 11)

In other words, transformational leaders are agents of change, both for individuals within the school and for the school as a whole. In a PLC, transformational leadership inspires high levels of commitment and motivation, as transformational leaders are able to develop models of collaborative practice that create high levels of collective responsibility. This in turn establishes a culture of innovation in which staff members feel secure enough to take risks and trial new ideas.

Yet becoming a change agent is not as simple as it sounds. It is inevitable that even the most courageous of PLC leaders will experience some degree of discomfort, disagreement, or resistance to the process; after all, change often challenges deeply held beliefs, and "even the most assertive of teachers can be fearful of change" (Fullan, 2008, p. 61). As John Kenneth Galbraith (1971) says, "Faced with the choice between changing one's mind and proving that there is no need to do so, almost everyone gets busy on the proof." In response, Fullan (2001) proposes that change agents don't "live more peacefully, but . . . they can handle more uncertainty—and conflict—and are better at working through complex issues in ways that energize rather than deplete the commitment of the organizational members" (p. 15).

## FLEXIBILITY

This responsibility refers to the extent to which leaders can adapt to the needs of a changing situation, are comfortable with dissent, and can see things from different perspectives. The specific behaviors and characteristics associated with this responsibility are as follows:

- Adapting one's leadership style to the needs of specific situations
- Being directive or nondirective as the situation warrants
- Encouraging people to express diverse and opposing opinions
- Being comfortable with making major changes in how things are done (Marzano et al., 2005, p. 49)

Flexibility refers to the degree to which leaders adjust their leadership style to account for the current reality and to manage conflict. Like the change agent responsibility, this responsibility is associated with transformational leadership. Transformational leaders use flexibility to help people adapt in order to meet mutual goals. They emphasize communication, positive relationships, support, and accountability (Muhammad & Hollie, 2012).

In creating a shared understanding and common language, PLC leaders re-envisage collegial conflict as critical to growth. They spend time developing a culture in which courageous conversations are introduced, practiced, and then embedded into the school's culture.

## IDEALS AND BELIEFS

This responsibility refers to a leader's role in shaping the ideals and beliefs that underpin the mission and vision of the school (see commitment 4). The specific behaviors and characteristics associated with this responsibility are as follows:

- Committing to well-defined beliefs about schools, teaching, and learning
- Sharing beliefs about school, teaching, and learning with the staff
- Aligning behaviours so that they are consistent with beliefs (Marzano et al., 2005, p. 51)

In the words of businessman Max De Pree (1989), "Practice without belief is a forlorn existence" (p. 55). If human beings are at their best when they operate from a set of strong ideals and beliefs (Marzano et al., 2005), then shared values are a key element of effective PLCs, and it is the leader's responsibility to foster and promote these values. The question of ideals and beliefs in a PLC goes back to the issue of school culture—discussed in commitment 1—as the ideas and beliefs that typify a conventional school must be modified in order to create the schoolwide culture of collaboration necessary to propel the PLC process.

## INTELLECTUAL STIMULATION

This responsibility refers to the extent to which the school leader ensures that all staff members are aware of the most current theories and practices regarding effective learning. The specific behaviors and characteristics associated with this responsibility are as follows:

- Continually exposing staff to contemporary research and theory on effective schooling
- Keeping informed about current research and theory on effective schooling
- Fostering systematic discussion regarding current research and theory on effective schooling (Marzano et al., 2005, p. 53)

The responsibility of intellectual stimulation requires PLC leaders to ensure that all members of staff are familiar with the latest research and theory pertaining to quality teaching, as discussions around these topics are an integral part of PLC culture. For Fullan (2001), this responsibility involves "knowledge building, knowledge sharing, knowledge creation [and] knowledge management" (p. 77). Leaders who prioritize intellectual stimulation deliberately and regularly weave discussions on contemporary research into their everyday interactions with the school community.

Education writer and consultant Larry Lashway (2001) sees the exposure of staff to new knowledge as a key driver of the change process, explaining that "deep changes require deep learning, and leaders must build teacher learning into the everyday fabric of school life" (p. 7). Marzano and his colleagues (2016) have argued that distributed knowledge, collective capacity, and shared responsibility are a more powerful catalyst for improvement than the abilities of the best teachers working in isolation, while additional research indicates:

> A school's social capital—the connections between educators and the extent to which they exchange and build on each other's knowledge—is just as powerful a predictor of student achievement as raw human capital—the skills of individual teachers. (National Center for Literacy Education, 2013, p. 4)

As this evidence suggests, it is critical for PLC leaders to ensure that even the most controversial new ideas are discussed and shared collaboratively, as it is through this collective process that theory can be transformed into practice.

## KNOWLEDGE OF CURRICULUM, INSTRUCTION, AND ASSESSMENT

This responsibility refers to the extent to which the school leader is a leader of learning. The specific behaviors and characteristics associated with this responsibility are as follows:

- Possessing extensive knowledge about effective instructional practices
- Possessing extensive knowledge about effective curricular practices
- Possessing extensive knowledge about effective assessment practices
- Providing conceptual guidance regarding effective classroom practices (Marzano et al., 2005, p. 55)

Knowledge of curriculum, instruction, and assessment is a key responsibility in a PLC, since a PLC leader's primary role "is the guidance and direction of instructional improvement" (Elmore, 2000, p. 13). In addition to taking a transformational approach to leadership, successful PLC leaders are also instructional leaders: they focus on the direct impact of teacher practice on student outcomes. In the words of Viviane Robinson, Margie Hohepa, and Claire Lloyd (2009), "Instructional leadership establishes an academic mission; provides feedback on teaching and learning; and promotes professional development" (p. 88). In order to fulfill the goal of improving outcomes for every student, instructional leaders are required to both cultivate a comprehensive understanding of curriculum, instruction, and assessment and to use this knowledge to guide classroom practice. As Robinson (2006) maintains, school leaders "cannot competently and confidently lead instructional improvement, even with substantial delegation of responsibilities, without in-depth and up-to-date knowledge of at least one curriculum area" (p. 72).

## MONITORING AND EVALUATING

This responsibility refers to how the leader uses evidence and data to ensure that the direction in which the school is headed results in tangible improvements in student learning. The specific behaviors and characteristics associated with this responsibility are as follows:

- Continually monitoring the effectiveness of the school's curricular, instructional, and assessment practices
- Being continually aware of the impact of the school's practices on student achievement (Marzano et al., 2005, p. 56)

The concept of monitoring and accountability is not new. Too often, however, accountability has been imposed on schools from the outside in the form of school inspections and standardized tests. In fact, the most effective form of accountability occurs when professionals engage in self-assessment and then actively take steps to bring about improvement. The responsibility of monitoring and evaluating stipulates that it is a PLC leader's role to monitor the extent to which school practices have an effect on student achievement. This form of accountability requires strong commitment and a clear vision: "The more understood, accepted, and cohesive the culture of a school, the better able it is to move in concert toward ideals it holds and objectives it wishes to pursue" (Sergiovanni, 1984, p. 9).

## OPTIMIZER

This responsibility refers to the extent to which the school leaders inspire others and act as a driving force behind the implementation of challenging innovations. The specific behaviors and characteristics associated with this responsibility are as follows:

- Inspiring teachers to accomplish things that might be beyond their grasp
- Being the driving force behind major initiatives
- Portraying a positive attitude about the ability of staff to accomplish substantial things (Marzano et al., 2005, p. 56)

The transformation that the PLC process sets in motion is impossible to achieve unless a significant group of stakeholders within the school believes that useful change is possible.

Without a compelling vision, a transformational effort can dissolve into a fragmented list of confusing projects that take the school in the wrong direction or nowhere at all. In failed school improvement, there are often plenty of plans and programs but no vision, leaving teachers confused and alienated. Sometimes leaders do have a sense of direction, but they communicate it to staff in a way that is too complicated or obscure to be useful.

Research suggests that optimism is a critical characteristic of an effective school leader. As Kenneth Leithwood, Christopher Day, Pam Sammons, Alma Harris, and David Hopkins (2006) note, "School leaders improve teaching and learning indirectly and most powerfully through their influence on staff motivation, commitment and working conditions" (p. 10). The school leader commonly sets the emotional tone in a school, developing an environment where "new ideas and innovation abound" (Blase & Kirby, 2000, p. 5). While it may not be easy to maintain an optimistic vision in the face of staff skepticism or resistance, successful PLC leaders have the courage to stick with their vision and take the necessary steps to achieve high levels of learning for all students.

# REFLECTION

PLC leadership is not easy. It takes commitment. Second-order change—the change required to transform schools in order to improve learning for all students—requires courage and relentless focus. As Fritz (1984) explains, talk without action is:

> often employed by people who "hold the vision" while ignoring what is going on around them. These are the idle dreamers who give real visionaries a bad name. Not to confuse a creator with a dreamer. Dreamers only dream, but creators bring their dreams into reality. Only an accurate awareness of reality and an accurate awareness of your vision will enable you to form structural tension as an important part of the creative process. (p. 118)

This is far from easy to do—but the struggle and effort is worth it! The following scenario illustrates the significance of courageous, focused school leadership in driving whole-school improvement.

> The principal, assistant principal, and two teacher-leaders from a small primary school attend a conference on transforming collaboration. As a result of the sessions they attend, they are inspired to introduce the concept of PLC transformation to their school. As they discuss their experiences at the conference, the leaders find themselves drawn to the key tenets of a PLC, particularly the belief that all students can achieve the required standard through a collaborative approach in which educators take collective responsibility for addressing curriculum, assessment, and instructional challenges.
>
> *continued* →

At the first leadership team meeting upon their return, the team sits down to discuss the most effective way of building shared understanding and generating excitement among school staff in order to commence the PLC journey. They begin by examining their school's existing mission statement, which they have spent some time constructing, and quickly realize that it isn't aligned to PLC principles. The statement reads, "Our mission is to build a supportive learning community where all students are challenged to take responsibility for their own learning."

The leadership team notes that the statement is ambiguous and doesn't really emphasize the PLC tenets that resonated with them at the conference. On the contrary, the way that the statement is worded actually gives teachers the opportunity to abdicate responsibility for the learning of their students. The more the team examines the school's mission statement, the more it comes to realize that the beliefs it contains have pervaded the entire school community, to damaging effect. Some of the students are failing, and some of the teachers show little concern about whether all their students are learning at a high level.

The leadership team realizes that it needs to work on shaping the school's mission and values so that they align with contemporary research on student learning. Once the leadership team has reached consensus on this first step of their PLC journey, it considers the actions that will help the staff to get on board with the coming transformation. After careful planning and in-depth discussion, the team agrees to:

- Share with other staff members their experiences at the conference and their own individual perspectives about why they are excited by the possibilities of becoming a PLC

- Collate and present to staff school-level and team-level student-learning data that represent the school's current reality

- Present key pieces of research to staff to raise awareness and promote informed discussion

- Share data-based case studies to enlighten staff about why the PLC process is so powerful

- Emphasize how the PLC process will link with structures already existing at the school, particularly in relation to the work teams are doing on teaching practice and curriculum alignment

The leadership team agrees that it will use the next staff meeting to explain why it is essential to revise the school's mission statement through the PLC lens. It also decides to allocate time after the initial whole-staff session to meet with each member of staff individually. In these individual meetings, the leadership team will explore staff members' attitudes toward the changes necessitated by the PLC process and identify any areas of difficulty. With staff consent, the team will collate and use this information to support the formation of an implementation strategy that it will share with staff for further feedback. The leadership team commits to act on this feedback while remaining true to the PLC process.

In introducing staff to the challenge of becoming a PLC, the leaders at this school display their willingness to embrace second-order change. They establish a connection between the beliefs of the PLC work and the school's existing beliefs. They consider the importance of getting staff excited, inspired, and committed as a key part of the implementation plan. They include genuine opportunities for staff to have input into the process with the objective of building collective ownership. They ensure that they have drawn on current research to build a rationale for doing this work. The leaders consciously make links to teaching and learning practices that are already happening within the school. They use the school's learning data to articulate a case for change and make sure to monitor the staff's reaction through the inclusion of individual meeting time. As a result, there is little doubt that this school will experience a smooth and successful transition from conventional school to PLC-in-progress.

# REFLECTIVE QUESTIONS: COMMITMENT 2—FIND THE COURAGE YOU NEED TO LEAD

As you consider each reflective question, contemplate your response and identify the evidence that supports your thinking.

## ACTION 2.1: FIND THE COURAGE TO CHALLENGE CONVENTION

- To what extent do your school's existing policies, words, and actions align with the belief that all students can learn at high levels?

- Do staff at your school believe that all students can learn at high levels? If not, how can you change their minds?

## ACTION 2.2: FIND THE COURAGE TO COMMIT TO GROWTH

- What school improvement factors do you associate with all students being able to achieve at high levels? How could you adapt or modify these factors in your school?

- Where is your school on the five-level HRS framework? What more can you do to grow your school into a High Reliability School?

## ACTION 2.3: FIND THE COURAGE TO FOCUS ON WHAT WORKS

- How can school leaders create a culture of innovation in which staff members feel secure enough to take risks and trial new ideas to improve teaching and learning?

- What is your role in ensuring staff members are aware of the most current theories and practices regarding effective learning?

- Which of the seven responsibilities for second-order change best describes your approach as a leader? Which one do you need to work on most?

# INSIGHTS FROM THE FIELD

*When I served as curriculum coordinator before we started the PLC process, I was trying to push all these planners and telling the staff, "You should be thinking about this, and you should have knowledge of this." But now, the teams are doing that themselves. They're saying, "We need to get out the curriculum, we need to pick out the important parts of it, we need to understand it." And it's more our role as leaders to say, "How can we support you?"—which is so much nicer than feeling like you're hitting your head against a brick wall.*

*As a leadership team, we need to help collaborative teams understand what it means to work as a team and support leaders to work alongside their colleagues. It's really, really important for leaders to actually be part of the team, to actually be in there. In fact, leader is probably a bad choice of words.*

**—AMELIA, ASSISTANT PRINCIPAL**

*The reason we started this journey in the first place was that we leaders were introducing lots of good things to help build teacher capacity, but our staff members weren't taking us up on it because they felt like they knew everything. Whereas the PLC process appeals to their core beliefs and makes them more likely to want to take it up. For example, one of our school leaders was creating time for teachers to go and visit other classes to look at good practice, and no one wanted to do it, then we got to the review and we were asking about that piece: "Nah, I haven't had time, I haven't been able to fit that in." The difference now is that the teachers are paying attention to the data and using them to identify what they want to improve on. Which has meant they are now asking to go and observe someone else. Thanks to the PLC process, they're seeing a reason for the professional learning. And these observations are actually driving some of the things we were wanting teachers to focus on.*

**—DREW, PRINCIPAL**

*I feel that if you build a momentum in the PLC journey, it's like a snowball going down a hill and people tend to get consumed by it. Yes, it will divert off at times, and sometimes it needs to divert off for short conversations around other things. But if you can keep re-addressing the issue by asking the right question—"How does that help with student learning?"—it seems to be that the snowball will roll in the right direction as it's going down the hill. It doesn't veer off for very long.*

**—CHRIS, PRINCIPAL**

# C H A P T E R  3
# Build a Climate of Trust

*Transformation begins with trust. Trust is the essential link between leaders and led, vital to people's job satisfaction and loyalty, vital to followership. It is doubly important when organizations are seeking rapid improvement, which requires exceptional effort and competence, and doubly again to organizations like schools that offer few extrinsic motivators (money, status, power). And it is as fragile as it is precious; once damaged, it is nearly impossible to repair.*

—Robert Evans

Central to the transformation of a school into a PLC is the establishment of a culture that centers on trust. Building trust in a PLC requires leaders to take deliberate actions that are intimately linked to the core work of achieving high levels of learning for all students. In our discussion of commitment 3, we will outline some of the high-leverage actions that effective PLC leaders take to create a climate of relational trust within their organizations.

Anthony S. Bryk and Barbara Schneider (2002) explain relational trust in the following way:

> A complex web of social exchanges conditions the basic operations of schools. Embedded in the daily social routines of schools is an interrelated set of mutual dependencies among all key actors: students, teachers, principals and administrators, and parents. These structural dependencies create feelings of vulnerability for the individuals involved. . . . Relational trust views the social exchanges of schooling as organized around a distinct set of role relationships: teachers with students, teachers with other teachers, teachers with parents and with their school principal. Each party in a role relationship maintains an understanding of his or her role obligations and holds some expectations about the role obligations of the other. (p. 20)

Given that so much of a PLC's success depends on the willingness of school staff members to deprivatize their practice with one another, it follows that without high levels of relational trust, it will be effectively impossible to build a network of high-functioning collaborative teams. Conversely, as educator and author Stephen Covey (2004) writes, "When the trust account is high, communication is easy, instant, and effective" (p. 188). One of the critical commitments that PLC leaders must make is to understand the importance of trust in a collaborative culture and build the necessary conditions for trust to flourish.

Collaborative teams are the bedrock of PLCs, so let us consider for a moment the work that these teams undertake. Teams of teachers get together on a regular basis to analyze data related to the impact their teaching has had on student learning. Now, imagine that you are a teacher on this team, and the results you bring to the table are the lowest in terms of student achievement. It is likely that you would want to be in an environment where your colleagues had your best interests at heart, and where the focus was not on you as an individual but rather on collective responsibility for ensuring that all students learn.

As this example demonstrates, working within a safe psychological space in which we can share openly our successes and failures, fears and hopes, and strengths and weaknesses is paramount to determining whether a PLC culture will thrive or merely survive. Building relationships in the absence of trust is a bit like driving a car without fuel: you can sit in the vehicle for as long as you like, but it's not going to take you very far.

# KEY ACTIONS

To explicate commitment 3, we will outline three key actions that leaders need to support in order to successfully build trust among all the key stakeholders in a PLC.

- **ACTION 3.1:** Build behaviors that promote trust.
- **ACTION 3.2:** Build bridges to repair trust.
- **ACTION 3.3:** Build authenticity in your interactions.

## ACTION 3.1: BUILD BEHAVIORS THAT PROMOTE TRUST

Our explanation of action 3.1 draws from the foundational research of Bryk and Schneider (2002). These researchers looked closely at the correlation between trust in schools and student achievement, and what they found is very useful when it comes to identifying the trustworthy traits that leaders of a PLC would benefit from adopting. Leaders need to be aware of the lenses that people use to determine whether a person is trustworthy and ensure that their deliberate actions support the development of collegial trust.

Bryk and Schneider (2002) describe the lenses through which we observe and interpret the behavior of others as *criteria for discernment*. Essentially, one uses these criteria in a school setting to determine whether or not a person might be trustworthy. According to Bryk and Schneider (2002), there are four criteria for discernment.

1. Integrity

2. Respect

3. Competence

4. Personal regard

## INTEGRITY

In the context of leadership within a PLC, *integrity* is defined as consistency between what leaders say and what they do. In a deeper sense, integrity also implies that an ethical perspective guides the PLC leaders' work, ensuring that their actions and behaviors are all oriented toward maximizing the learning of all students. In order to illustrate how this might look, we share the story of one principal's endeavors to reculture his school as a PLC.

Ted is the principal of a secondary school that has pledged to transform into a PLC. Over three consecutive staff meetings during the first term of the school year, he attempts to show his staff how to formulate SMART (strategic and specific, measurable, attainable, results oriented, and time bound; Conzemius & O'Neill, 2014) goals in their weekly collaborative team meetings. By the conclusion of the third meeting, Ted feels that he has thoroughly covered the key aspects of this strategy, so he directs each team to devise at least one SMART goal of its own by the end of the second term.

Ted has repeatedly assured his staff members that they should let him know if they need additional support, as it will be important to take things slowly and strategically while they all learn how to work collaboratively as a PLC. After the meeting, the staff members confer and realize that they do not feel ready to progress to SMART goals. Some of the teams are still struggling to develop a shared understanding of the curriculum, and most consider the introduction of SMART goals to be premature at best. Based on Ted's repeated assurances, two of the heads of department in the school decide to meet with him to discuss their concerns.

When the heads of department share some of their concerns, Ted listens. However, contrary to his earlier statements, he refuses to change his expectation that each team will have a SMART goal by the end of the second term. What's more, his staff finds out after the meeting that Ted is scheduled to present the following week at a regional conference about his school's success in becoming a PLC—and part of his brief is to talk about how his teams are using SMART goals.

It is likely that as a result of Ted's actions, some staff members will feel that his behavior as principal lacked integrity. The inconsistency between his words and actions and the lack of flexibility he shows supports this perception, as could the presumption that he is advancing his own interests rather than those of staff or students. It is important to note that while Ted's actions may be well intentioned, staff could still perceive his integrity to be lacking. With some slight changes to his approach, however, Ted could easily demonstrate more integrity and increase the likelihood that others will find him a trustworthy leader:

When two of his heads of department share some of the staff's concerns about rushing into SMART goals, Ted listens, empathizes, and asks them what they consider to be a more realistic time line. He also checks in with the rest of the staff about their feelings and offers to attend some of their next meetings to get a better sense of the development of the teams.

The staff are aware that Ted is going to present at a regional principals' conference the following week on what his school has done in their journey toward becoming a PLC. Part of his brief is to talk about how his teams are using SMART goals. Ted asks the staff whether he can take some team facilitators with him to share in his presentation. He specifically requests his staff to share how the teams view SMART goals in terms of their contribution to the development of a school culture that genuinely is focused on student and staff learning.

This course of action shows that the Ted is people centered in his approach and responsive to the needs of his staff. He shows integrity by acknowledging the value of the input from his colleagues while staying focused on the vision and direction of the school, which in turn enhances staff members' trust in their principal.

## RESPECT

People who consistently display respect for others are more likely to be viewed as trustworthy. Leaders need to model and develop this important component of trust if the school is to transform into a high-functioning PLC. By demonstrating respect, PLC leaders acknowledge the important role that each staff member plays in educating students and the ways in which everyone in the school community must depend on each other.

Active and genuine listening is a key indication that educators have the kind of respect for their colleagues that can foster mutual understanding. To show how this might look from a leader's perspective, consider Linda's challenge to effectively lead her collaborative team:

Linda, a collaborative team facilitator, is holding a meeting of her eighth-grade English team, which consists of herself and four other teachers. To open the meeting, Linda nominates a minute-taker who will be responsible for recording the meeting. She begins by reminding everyone of the norm that she wants them to focus on—"Listen with the intention to understand rather than just be understood"—and asks them to remain cognizant of it during discussions.

Next, Linda hands out data from a recent student assessment along with a set of questions for the team members to answer. She reads out each question and sets a five-minute timer to ensure that team members are using time efficiently. In order to hear all team members' responses, she grants each member of the team a turn to speak, and she makes a rule that no one may speak for more than one minute of the allocated five minutes.

Linda concludes the meeting with an open question about the norm: "How do you think we did today with our norm?" The team members mumble something vague in the affirmative, and then the four other teachers quickly adjourn to the parking lot without Linda for a proper debriefing. Despite Linda's best efforts to be inclusive, respectful of time constraints, and focused on the learning, many team members still feel uneasy about the meetings and don't fully trust in her leadership.

As a result of Linda's strict approach to team facilitation, some staff members may have felt a lack of professional respect. For mutual respect to flourish, it is important for Linda to know that others on the team share the same concerns that she does. It is also important for the team members to know that their thoughts are genuinely sought after and valued, even when there is disagreement on an issue. With just some slight changes to her approach, Linda could increase the likelihood that others find her to be a trustworthy team facilitator:

Linda reads out each question and sets a five-minute timer to ensure that the team is using its time efficiently. In order to hear all team members give their responses, she grants each member of the team a turn to speak, and she makes a rule that no one may speak for more than one minute of the allocated five minutes. At the conclusion of the allocated time, Linda invites anyone in the group to summarize what they believe to be the common elements in the discussion and explain what they feel the team needs to commit to over the next three weeks of the learning cycle. Once the team members have responded, Linda thanks them and tells them she will incorporate their ideas into the pacing guide that they will work from over the next three weeks.

She concludes the meeting with an open question about the norm: "How do you think the norm is serving us in our work as a collaborative team, and do you have suggestions about how we might continue to enhance our professional dialogue?" After listening to her team's suggestions, she incorporates them into the next meeting.

## COMPETENCE

A hallmark of PLCs is the commitment by all staff members to view themselves as learners. Staff in a PLC are open to changing their practices in the pursuit of higher levels of learning for all students. In a PLC, it is the school leader's responsibility to ensure that staff understand the key competencies that educators require to fulfill their changing role.

Competence is demonstrated by the ability to achieve desired outcomes, including not only learning goals for students but also effective work conditions for PLC teachers and leaders. It is safe to assume that teachers, parents, and leaders make judgments regarding issues of competence on a regular basis. One key to building relational trust is an ongoing commitment by school staff to commit to ongoing improvement of student learning.

There are a number of competencies that serve school leaders well in their efforts to transform their schools into PLCs. In the following list, we offer seven of the most important competencies.

1. Being a productive team member

2. Taking responsibility

3. Committing to the PLC ideal

4. Displaying social and emotional awareness

5. Developing organizational skills

6. Seeking information and facts

7. Being a problem solver

We explain these important competencies in the following sections.

### Being a Productive Team Member

Working at becoming a highly effective team member is an important competency that school leaders need to both develop and model. PLCs that flourish require teams to work at their optimum level. Drawing from the work of psychologist Susan A. Wheelan (2013), following are key actions and attitudes school leaders need to be aware of so that they can support collaborative team members to build trust.

- Competent team members are present. Not only do they turn up physically to meetings, they turn up cognitively.

- Competent team members commit to learning about team development and recognize where they are in their journey. They embrace the review of their team's progress as an opportunity to grow and refine their collaborative practice.

- Competent team members are patient. Genuine and sustainable change takes time, and while being clear about one's work is critical (see commitment 5), so is the ability to consider things thoughtfully and strategically.

- Competent team members make peace with not knowing how to do things. They embrace the unknown as an opportunity to inquire and learn.

- Competent team members expect there to be differences of opinion and see conflict as a sign the school is moving forward in its development as a PLC. Trusted team members can be relied on to listen to other viewpoints and use the difference of opinions as a way to reach consensus.

- Competent team members don't personalize issues. They focus on the things that make the biggest difference to student learning.

- Competent team members understand and model the ability to negotiate, mediate, and compromise on issues related to teaching and learning.

- Competent team members take responsibility for their role within the team. They do what is asked of them, from analyzing data to adhering to behavioral standards.

- Competent team members support other team members, even when they do not agree with them. Because they focus their energies on the purpose of the work, competent team members ensure they are as committed to growing their own collaborative abilities as they are those of others.

- Competent team members complete their tasks on time and when needed. They know that delivering on their commitments in a timely fashion is critical if the team is to respond to student and community needs in real time.

- Competent team members are willing to reflect on the workings of the team. They are able to confront truths and embrace them as an opportunity to learn. They can do so respectfully.

We can't stress strongly enough the need for school leaders to be proactive in developing their understanding of the competencies that team members need. This aids leaders in supporting educators to become increasingly more productive in their collaborative efforts. Just organizing educators into teams doesn't mean that they will automatically have the ability to function in a team. The role of the school leader is to strengthen educators' ability to work in the manner required to be a high-functioning PLC, and both monitor and support their efforts to do this.

## Taking Responsibility

School leaders need to ensure team members have the will, skills, and knowledge necessary to take collective responsibility for student learning. In our experience, a team is far more likely to be successful when the members within it trust one another to share in this responsibility and work interdependently to fulfill it. It might be as simple as a school leader collecting data from each team's reflection sheet and collating the data so that staff can analyze it at the next meeting. Another example of leadership support involves a team leader bringing to the team the collation of the data from each grade level so members can examine it through their data protocol (see commitment 5). School leaders need to carefully consider how they can strengthen team members' ability to contribute toward the achievement of the school's and team's goals.

## Committing to the PLC Ideal

Of all the schools we have worked in and researched, a common thread of success is the commitment both leader and teachers make to the PLC work. As explained in chapter 2 (page 15), outcomes are more likely to be achieved when leaders commit to second-order change through an unwavering belief that all students can learn at high levels.

Commitment is also displayed when teachers collaborate willingly and with a genuine spirit of inquiry. When they can trust that other staff members are equally committed to the ideals of PLC work, teachers will persist in their collaborative efforts even when the work becomes murky and difficult. School leaders play a vital role in modeling their commitment to the PLC ideal through the support they provide to teams and the work they undertake on a daily basis.

## Displaying Social and Emotional Awareness

At the heart of PLCs is collaboration, and it is the leader's role to continue to strengthen educators' understanding of the behaviors required to successfully collaborate. Collaboration is a human enterprise that requires numerous social and emotional behaviors. We are all different, and during collaborative meetings, these differences can unite us or divide us.

Through the development of *norms*—collective commitments that prescribe how team members will behave during meetings—teams commit to raising their awareness of the social and emotional skills each member will need to bring to the table. They understand that the way they use the time they have will play a significant role in the education of their students. With that awareness comes a propensity to check in on themselves and one another as they engage in conversations that are designed to increase student and teacher learning. It may be that staff learn how to set aside unproductive patterns of listening, responding, and inquiring or how to aim for consensus when it comes to decision-making processes. Ultimately, an effective PLC challenges staff members to look in the mirror, rather than through the window, when it comes to the interpersonal skills they wish to seek and develop.

## Developing Organizational Skills

Schools must be able to organize themselves at multiple levels to successfully implement and review the work of a PLC. Commitment 4 offers many insights on this topic. While those on staff who thrive on high-level organization are drawn on in a PLC to guide teamwork and tasks, it is still the school leader's responsibility to oversee all organizational matters. Consider for the moment some of the work of high-level collaborative teams.

- Developing and reviewing norms
- Structuring and developing learning-focused agendas
- Setting and reviewing SMART goals
- Understanding and incorporating the use of data and discussion protocols
- Collecting, collating, and presenting various types of student achievement data
- Engaging in purposeful and structured staff conferences
- Adopting, refining, or creating common assessment tasks
- Creating and reviewing proficiency scales
- Creating and shaping the guaranteed and viable curriculum
- Managing timetables for both core instruction and intervention
- Collecting and analyzing work samples
- Collecting and organizing both obtrusive and unobtrusive assessments

As you can see from this list—and it's not an exhaustive one—there are many tasks individuals and teams carry out that require attention to detail, time management, high-level communication, and commitment. Great leaders recognize this and ensure those on collaborative teams use their strengths for the benefit of student learning by deliberately fostering organizational skills. These skills are an indicator of competence, and therefore a driver of relational trust.

## Seeking Information and Facts

One hallmark of PLCs is the use of facts rather than opinions when making instructional decisions related to student learning. School leaders need to carefully monitor and intervene when necessary to ensure that collaborative teams have the skills and understandings necessary to base their decision making on facts.

In a PLC, competent team members are always looking for evidence of the effect their teaching practices, programs, and decisions have had on student learning. Although it sounds simple, this is often one of the key indicators missing from team dialogue in schools. The imperative to rely only on facts can be very problematic for schools that have a history of making policy and program decisions based on perception, opinion, personal preference, and positional power.

Consider a team that feels great about teaching a unit of work on the California gold rush due to high student engagement and real-world connections drawn from the students. Competency is defined by the difference this approach makes to student learning—so while teacher satisfaction and student engagement are both important, a high-performing collaborative team would measure this perception against the data from ongoing common assessments and compare the results that the students achieved against the standards.

Looking for the truth in data can be a high-leverage strategy for change. The key to achieving competence in this area is for PLC leaders to ensure that collaborative teams constantly seek facts and information about the impact their teaching efforts have had on the level of student achievement in their classrooms.

### Being a Problem Solver

Finally, competency is evident when individuals can contribute to solving problems as opposed to merely identifying—or even creating—them. If PLC members are to embrace the spirit of collective inquiry, school leaders must empower collaborative teams to make their own decisions and forge their own direction, as long as it is consistent with the school's agreed-on mission and vision. Leaders need to ensure that team members are as good at asking the right questions during meetings as they are at advocating for their ideas to be heard.

As DuFour and his colleagues (2016) explain, the work of PLCs revolves around four critical questions, to which Marzano and colleagues (2016) add two additional fundamental questions.

1. What do we want students to learn? What is it we want our students to know?

2. How will we know if our students are learning?

3. How will we respond when students do not learn?

4. How will we enrich and extend the learning for students who are proficient?

5. How will we increase our instructional competence?

6. How will we coordinate our efforts as a school?

By their very nature, these questions lend themselves to an inquiry-based approach. The answers that collaborative teams come up with will vary from school to school and team to team, but every school leader and collaborative team member will find it useful to reflect on these questions and revisit them periodically to track the progress of the school. In a PLC, the real work isn't about doing more but in developing the ability to ask each other the right questions to explore. Leaders play an active role in ensuring these six questions underpin the work of each collaborative team in their school.

Leaders actively develop competent team members' ability to seek out answers that best meet the school's needs regarding curriculum, assessment, instruction, teacher development, and leadership. Leaders ensure collaborative teams do this by collectively agreeing to follow these guidelines.

- Always aim for consensus even when team members hold different views.

- Concentrate on the actions that are most likely to bring the best learning outcomes for students.

- Recognize that like students, teachers are lifelong learners.

## PERSONAL REGARD

Relational trust will deepen if staff perceive that their leader cares about them and will go the extra mile to help them, even if it is not in the leader's role to do so. Leaders need to be exemplars of this, emphasizing that their role is one of support in order to encourage the same habit in others. For example, a principal who takes a class so that the teacher can observe a colleague is demonstrating personal regard—or it could be something much smaller than this, such as allowing a staff member to use the photocopier first because he or she appears to be in a hurry.

To engender trust, it is essential that a PLC leader behaves like someone who generally cares about learning and other people, even in high-stress or conflictive situations. As an example, think about the following scenario.

A principal, Adam, is having a difficult time with a staff member, Patrick, who sees collaboration as a threat to his autonomy. Patrick has long been a high-performing teacher and views working collaboratively with others as a form of mentoring, which will take him away from his day-to-day duties. He is more focused on his individual needs than on the collective responsibility of the school community.

After many failed attempts to discuss the issue, Adam decides on a different approach. Next time he meets with Patrick, he tries it out:

> Patrick, I understand you have reservations about the fact that we have restructured the timetable in order to meet more often on matters related to learning. The reason for the change is actually simple. Now, like no other time in the history of education, the research is reaching a consensus. The evidence clearly shows that high-level collaboration makes a bigger difference to more kids more often. Unless the entire school community can learn to take collective responsibility for student learning, we will continue to see kids slip through the cracks.

*continued* →

I appreciate the value you bring to the school based on the outstanding results you get for your kids. You work hard to ensure that your own students achieve at high levels. But why should other students miss out on benefiting from the direct impact you could have on their teachers? At the core of this school is learning: learning for leaders, learning for teachers, and learning for students.

You may not feel you have as much to learn from your colleagues in terms of teaching, but I know you will learn a lot about what it takes to become an effective team member. Before I hear more from you about what you are struggling with, I want to let you know I will do whatever it takes to work with you to bring you into the collaborative space we are growing at this school. Our kids deserve no less.

Patrick still does not like what he is hearing, but he leaves the meeting knowing that Adam has the learning needs of students and staff at heart. Gradually, his newfound trust in his principal's leadership begins to change his attitude, and he eventually becomes one of the school's biggest advocates for the benefits of collaborative teams.

Any teacher would be hard pressed to question the values that are inherent in Adam's comments. He not only demonstrates that he has learning at the heart of his decision-making processes but also communicates how highly he values collaboration. Further, he offers to make it his personal mission to work with Patrick during the PLC transition. Because Adam explicitly recognizes the value of Patrick's contributions to the school, his words provide a foundation for the relational trust needed to build a collaborative culture.

Given that collaboration is foundational to the building of PLCs, leaders must make it their mission to cultivate trust across the school community. But what can leaders do when trust has been broken? How do they help team members develop skills to heal the wounds that a lack of trust can inflict on their collaborative efforts?

## ACTION 3.2: BUILD BRIDGES TO REPAIR TRUST

Human relationships are complex, as we all know from personal experience. Sometimes, whether intentionally or not, trust gets broken. Human relationship building can seem unfair, as it can take a long time to develop trust yet only an instant to break it. Even when you assume that underneath it all, your colleagues want to trust you and be trusted by you, things can go awry.

When trust is broken, it is imperative to repair it as soon as possible. In her foundational work *Trust Matters*, educational leadership professor Megan Tschannen-Moran (2004) identifies four strategies that can aid in repairing trust when it has been broken. These strategies offer a framework for leaders that they can use to assist collaborative team members when trust is compromised.

1. **ADMIT IT:** Take responsibility for what you have done to contribute to the situation. Be prepared to admit what your actions were and that they led to harm. Even if you feel that you've done nothing wrong, it's important to acknowledge that your actions were harmful for someone else.

2. **APOLOGIZE:** This involves not only apologizing for what you did but also expressing genuine remorse for the harm your actions have caused. You should make it clear that although you have apologized, you know that this doesn't make it right.

3. **ASK FORGIVENESS:** Ask for the opportunity to show that you can do things differently if you are given the chance. With luck, the person will be open to accepting the apology and approach future interactions in good faith.

4. **AMEND YOUR WAYS:** Both parties work in partnership to decide how to move forward. This requires identifying the actions or areas of the relationship that need modification and then acting on this understanding to do better in the future.

Prerequisites to being able to use these four strategies are the willingness to examine your role in the breakdown of trust and the courage to initiate the strategies with the person whose trust has been damaged. In our extensive work in schools, we often encourage staff to set aside the need to "own the outcome." All you can do is stay true to the process and have faith that it will contribute to the rebuilding of trust. The following scenario shows how the strategies we've described work in practice.

> Dana has upset a colleague, Jill, during a collaborative team meeting. It isn't the first time. Over the past six months, she has deliberately made life harder for Jill, her younger, less experienced team facilitator. The source of Dana's behavior is disappointment and resentment, as she also applied for the facilitator position and was passed over for her younger colleague. Some of her behaviors have been antagonistic, such as deliberately questioning Jill's decisions, speaking over her in meetings, and refusing to comply with her requests for data.
>
> Dana is alerted to the fact that Jill is significantly upset by her actions and is considering leaving the school. Dana is genuinely surprised by the impact of her behavior, as she had acted without thinking and never really considered the situation from Jill's perspective.
>
> *continued* →

In an effort to make amends for her behavior and regain the trust of her colleagues, Dana agrees to work through Tschannen-Moran's (2004) four strategies.

1. **ADMIT IT:** Dana admits that she has shown some unprofessional behaviors and that her actions have been harmful.

2. **APOLOGIZE:** Dana shares how terrible she feels that Jill has taken her behavior so much to heart. She explains that it was never her intention to victimize Jill or make her want to leave, and she mentions that her poor behavior has been more to do her own disappointment than anybody else's actions.

3. **ASK FORGIVENESS:** Jill accepts Dana's apology and outlines what she would like to see in the meetings as a result of this conflict. She explains that she doesn't expect Dana to agree on everything that they discuss but would appreciate some respect and professional courtesy. Dana agrees that this is what she will work on.

4. **AMEND YOUR WAYS:** Dana acts differently during collaborative team time and works hard at modifying her behaviors. Jill feels a genuine newfound respect for Dana, aided by a deeper understanding of where she is coming from.

Given the complexities inherent in the real world of human interaction, this approach may seem easier to read about than it is to act out in reality. However, in our work with schools, we have seen leadership teams actively model these strategies, discuss them in meetings, and promote them to staff. As school leaders know, the students whom educators serve have a lot to lose when staff can't learn how to resolve conflict and rebuild trust.

## ACTION 3.3: BUILD AUTHENTICITY IN YOUR INTERACTIONS

We've already discussed integrity through the lens of relational trust as part of action 3.1. Psychologist and educator Robert Evans (1996), however, takes it a step further:

Innovation can't live without trust, but it needs more than trust—it needs confidence. We cannot have trust in those we distrust, but we do not necessarily have confidence in all those we trust. Some people whose sincerity and honesty are beyond reproach lack the capacity to translate their goals into reality. . . . Their heart, as we say, is in the right place, but they lack something that makes us follow them. To transform schools, principals and superintendents must inspire such confidence along with trust.

> The key to both is authenticity. Leaders who are followed are authentic; that is, they are distinguished not by their techniques or styles but by their integrity and their savvy. (p. 184)

Evans (1996) suggests that trust is an outcome of being authentic. In *Strengthening the Heartbeat: Leading and Learning Together in Schools*, Sergiovanni (2005) provides a list of the principles that leaders must commit to if they are to cultivate the authenticity that is needed to prompt meaningful transformative action.

- **ALL STUDENTS CAN LEARN GIVEN THE RIGHT CONDITIONS:** In a PLC, this principle is demonstrated when leaders move beyond rhetoric and into action. PLC leaders don't accept failure as an outcome for students. They know that while students will differ in their academic and social entry points, the core reason for the school's existence is to provide systems, structures (see chapter 4, page 55), and approaches to ensure students don't slip through the cracks.

- **STUDENTS CAN TAKE RESPONSIBILITY FOR THEIR OWN LEARNING IF WE GET THE STUDENT-TEACHER ROLE AND OTHER IMPORTANT ROLES SET RIGHT:** In a PLC, this principle is demonstrated when leaders view establishing collaborative teams that serve the needs of students as central to their role. The structures that leaders put in place optimize the chances for educators to be successful in their work and for students to see learning as the core purpose of their school.

- **SCHOOLS CAN BE TRANSFORMED INTO CARING LEARNING COMMUNITIES:** In a PLC, this principle is demonstrated when leaders believe that the primary purpose of their work is to do what is best for the students. Effective PLC leaders closely monitor the impact of what they do on student progress, and they foster a collaborative environment of mutual respect and support to ensure networks are established for the purpose of higher levels of learning.

- **UNDER THE RIGHT CONDITIONS, TEACHERS WILL TAKE RESPONSIBILITY FOR THEIR OWN LEARNING:** In a PLC, this principle is demonstrated when leaders trust their staff. They believe that all staff want what's best for student learning. They operate from this premise to challenge, support, and enrich the professional lives of teachers. They use it as the basis of finding common ground when conflict arises and when they need to make important policy and program decisions. The assumption that underpins this belief is that when teachers are trusted, supported, and believed in, they are more likely to take responsibility for their own learning.

- **GIVEN THE OPPORTUNITY AND TRAINING, EVEN THE POOREST OF PARENTS CAN BE EFFECTIVE PARTNERS IN THE EDUCATION OF THEIR CHILDREN:** In a PLC, this principle is demonstrated when leaders see parents as resources rather than roadblocks in their student's education. They devise ways of developing and maintaining open channels of communication on the learning progress of their students and are eager to learn about each student from their parents' perspective.

- **IF WE PROVIDE ENOUGH SUPPORT TO STUDENTS, ALL WILL SUCCEED:** In a PLC, this principle is demonstrated when leaders commit to finding any possible way of aligning their efforts to support any student at risk of failing or disengaging from school. They inquire into the best ways their school can provide systems and structures at the classroom, team, and whole-school level to reduce any chance of student failure. They see the failure of a student as not only their own failure but also the whole school's. Leaders embrace the notion of collective responsibility for student learning that is so critical to the work of a PLC.

- **EVERY TEACHER CAN BE A LEADER IF THE CIRCUMSTANCES ARE RIGHT AND THE ISSUES SEEM IMPORTANT ENOUGH:** In a PLC, this principle is demonstrated when leaders view learning as the core purpose for everything they do. The issue of high levels of learning for both staff and students is important to everybody. Through this unified focus on learning, there is room for teachers to make decisions on learning policies and practices. Formal leaders create conditions within the school so that teachers truly become the leaders of learning.

In short, the most powerful leaders are those with a steadfast belief in PLC principles—what commitment 2 refers to as *the courage you need to lead*—that shines through in the ways they act and interact. In our experience, leaders who successfully achieve higher levels of learning through their collaborative efforts do so because their efforts aren't just seen as authentic but indeed *are* authentic.

# REFLECTION

Leaders of PLCs continually look for opportunities to forge professional relationships built on trust. Regardless of the challenges becoming a PLC brings, successful leaders are unwavering in their commitment to the students, teachers, and communities they serve. They are driven by their conviction to make sure all their staff believe *all* students can learn at high levels. They see the building of relational trust as integral to this. PLC leaders show humility. They show conviction. They show passion. They show they can learn. And above all else, they move beyond intent and into action.

# REFLECTIVE QUESTIONS: COMMITMENT 3—BUILD A CLIMATE OF TRUST

As you consider each reflective question, contemplate your response and identify the evidence that supports your thinking.

## ACTION 3.1: BUILD BEHAVIORS THAT PROMOTE TRUST

- On a scale of 1 to 10 (where 10 is the highest rating and 1 the lowest) what would you say is the level of relational trust in your school? Why would you give it this rating?
- In what ways might you demonstrate integrity to your colleagues in your work?
- In what ways might you demonstrate respect to your colleagues in your work?
- In what ways might you demonstrate competence to your colleagues in your work?
- In what ways might you demonstrate personal regard to your colleagues in your work?

## ACTION 3.2: BUILD BRIDGES TO REPAIR TRUST

- Think about a colleague with whom you would like to build greater trust. Which of the insights and strategies in this section could you apply to that relationship?

## ACTION 3.3: BUILD AUTHENTICITY IN YOUR INTERACTIONS

- As you read about the principles that leaders commit to when building a school culture of authenticity, which ones stand out to you?
- In terms of your own leadership style, which principles require further examination?

# INSIGHTS FROM THE FIELD

*You have to build that trust within a team, and for us as a school we had to build that trust first. You have to actually be open and explicit: "This is why we're doing what we're doing. We're doing it because we want to get our kids to learn." We can't be pretending that we're going to do something but then not actually do it.*

—IVY, ASSISTANT PRINCIPAL

*I trust the other members of my team. We've got our essential curriculum, we've got our power standards, and we know that we are all working off exactly the same planner. That's the trust: you know that they will be doing the right thing and you don't have to check up.*

*We feel that we can talk to one another, I think because we're open. My very first meeting that I had with the team, we talked about how when you disagree with someone and want to question something, you're not questioning the person, you're questioning the activity or concept that we're trying to deal with. You're not personally going after someone. I think that set the standard for the year.*

*Some of the other teams are struggling because one person feels that he or she is the leader and has to do all the work. Whereas in our team, we don't; we share it out. Even for administrative tasks such as organizing an excursion or something, I'll organize one part, and then I'll say to another team member, "Do you want to do that one?" And I can trust that he or she will do it.*

—JESSICA, SIXTH-GRADE TEACHER

*There's a lot of open communication in our team. We can ask, "Do you think this is going to be beneficial?" We've got that mutual respect where we can say to each other, "Well, perhaps not yet, but maybe we can use it in a couple of weeks once the children get the foundations." There's a lot of that productive communication.*

—KAREN, SPECIALIST TEACHER

*I think good teams are based on trust. And I think it's important to build trust into the leadership team so that the collaborative teams feel that when they come into a meeting they can be open and honest. Previously, the teams would just warn a teacher who wasn't keeping up with data collection and not actually talk to that person about it, whereas now they're starting to open up about those things.*

—DREW, PRINCIPAL

*We've got a very large group of first- and second-grade students. One of the fifth- and sixth-grade teachers came to a meeting and said, "I'm really concerned that you've got such a large group in first and second grade, and I don't think they are accessing enough support." As a result, the fifth- and sixth-grade team actually rearranged its timetable to allow one of the teachers to help us with intervention. That shows me that a PLC is not just about working in levels, it's working as a community—they saw a need, and straight away they did something about it. I think that was a really powerful thing to see happen in a school.*

—ALEX, FIRST-GRADE TEACHER

# CHAPTER 4

# Shape School Structures for Success

*Without . . . structures that promote continual learning, it is impossible to build a professional learning community.*

—Kristine Hipp and Jane Huffman

The transformation from school to PLC demands significant attention to *structures*—the organizational elements that make up a school—since structures support schools to run efficiently. When schools establish appropriate structures and processes, they maintain the environment required for a PLC to be effective. In contrast, when organizational supports are missing or weak, the result can be disorganization, unclear direction, limited time, haphazard processes, and a sense of fragmentation. Under such conditions, educators can become frustrated and the journey can stall. A lack of attention to organizational structures in a PLC can cause a disconnect between the stated mission of the school and the actions that educators can actually take to improve practice.

Progress in a PLC is impossible without the implementation of structures to support the work being done. Structural modifications are therefore critical in terms of establishing a strong foundation on which a successful PLC can grow and develop.

## KEY ACTIONS

To explain commitment 4, we will outline three key actions required of leaders to shape school structures and provide solid roots for the school's transformation to a PLC.

- **ACTION 4.1:** Connect structures and culture.
- **ACTION 4.2:** Change structures through school leadership.
- **ACTION 4.3:** Cultivate structures for a high-performing PLC.

## ACTION 4.1: CONNECT STRUCTURES AND CULTURE

When first hearing about the PLC approach, many educators mistakenly see it as just another improvement or reform initiative. However, a PLC should more rightly be viewed as a supportive framework that allows schools to continuously transform themselves through the increasing internal capacity of educators to improve student learning. Kenneth Leithwood and Karen Seashore Louis (1999) suggest that the task of school leaders is to develop an organization that has the culture and structures to productively and effectively respond to the seemingly endless proliferation of new initiatives. The culture and structures in a high-performing PLC ensure that the focus never shifts from high levels of learning for all students, no matter what new improvement initiatives arise.

Many failed school-improvement processes rely only on structural change for their implementation and fail to address the underlying cultural changes required for transformation. This is because, of the two, structures are visible and relatively easy to change compared to culture. In reality, however, culture and structures are interdependent. Each cultural change will require a corresponding change to a structural aspect of the school to ensure that the cultural change is embedded into the way the school operates.

The implementation of the PLC process requires a delicate dance between changes in culture and changes in structures. Without a choreographed approach, a school's culture and its structures can work against each other, often stalling or totally derailing the transformation of the school. Leaders in a PLC understand and respond to the symbiotic relationship between the school's culture and its structures. Because existing school structures are deeply intertwined with the existing school culture, it is vital that school leaders carefully consider not only which structures might need to be changed to support the establishment of the school as a PLC but also the reasons why those structures have been institutionalized in the way they have.

The structures required for a high-performing PLC are like the roots of a tree. Strong roots that are grounded in rich soil will allow the tree to flourish. Without strong roots or without good soil, the tree will die. Similarly, if the root-like structures of a PLC are supported by a rich, positive, and optimistic school culture, the school will flourish.

## ACTION 4.2: CHANGE STRUCTURES THROUGH SCHOOL LEADERSHIP

In a PLC, it is primarily the responsibility of school leaders to create the organizational infrastructure that will result in high levels of learning for all students. Melanie S. Morrissey (2000) argues that the part school leaders play in driving the creation of PLC structures is highly significant to the overall success of the transformation because their role gives them the ability and authority to make the necessary structural changes. Not only do school leaders build the context for the PLC work, they also build the required organizational structures and address any structural barriers that exist. From the beginning of the PLC journey, leaders must make it a priority to reorganize the school so that all endeavors, of all educators, are directed toward the achievement of learning at high levels for all students.

When commencing the PLC journey, leaders may be uncertain as to the changes required or daunted by the prospect of having to make changes to historically embedded school structures. However, as collaborative teams start to form and barriers are identified within existing structures, leaders in a PLC must support educators to adapt to the new way they are asking them to work. Leaders who support educators through the creation of supportive structures ensure that they are establishing the foundations for collaboration. Then, as a school proceeds further down the PLC path, an important aspect of the school leader's role is to monitor and adjust the structural organization of the school in order to keep abreast of cultural changes and support continued transformation.

Each school is different, and so school structures will vary according to the school context. One constant, however, is that PLC leaders must build and adapt school structures in ways that promote interdependence and collaboration. Valirie Lee, Julia Smith, and Robert Croninger (1995) find that schools that implemented structural changes involving reduced hierarchy and increased collaboration had higher achievement rates and smaller achievement gaps than schools with a more conventional structure. Alongside a schoolwide culture of collaboration, structures that support collaboration must be established in order for a PLC to develop and flourish.

For leaders undertaking the PLC journey, two messages are clear.

1. Certain foundational structures must be in place to facilitate the development of a PLC.

2. Ongoing attention and adjustments must be made to structural and organizational arrangements as educators' capacity to work in a PLC continues to develop and flourish.

## ACTION 4.3: CULTIVATE STRUCTURES FOR A HIGH-PERFORMING PLC

The collaborative learning-focused culture that PLC leaders are trying to establish is at once demonstrated and supported by the structural changes that leaders undertake in their schools. Through structural modifications, leaders of PLCs build the infrastructure to allow PLCs to take root and grow. But which structures are most deserving of a school leaders' attention? Our experience has led us to identify the following primary areas on which PLC leaders may need to reflect.

- Structures to develop school mission and vision statements
- Structures that promote distributed leadership
- Structures for schoolwide communication

- Structures to ensure effective collaborative teams
- Structures that maximize student learning
- Structures for celebrating PLC progress

It should be noted that the structures required to establish a high-functioning PLC are not discrete, nor do they exist in a vacuum. Just as the culture and structures in a PLC are symbiotic, the structures themselves impact one another. When you change one structure to progress the work of the PLC, others will be affected and require further alteration. Ultimately, continued school improvement means continuous school change.

## STRUCTURES TO DEVELOP SCHOOL MISSION AND VISION STATEMENTS

One of the foremost considerations when transforming a school into a PLC is the development of the school's mission and vision statements (DuFour et al., 2016).

- The school's *mission statement* answers the fundamental questions of why the school exists and what it is trying to achieve. It clearly articulates to all stakeholders the school's fundamental purpose. The mission statement inspires educators in the work they do on a daily basis.
- The school's *vision statement* describes what the school must become to achieve its mission. It guides the transformations that must occur to move the school closer to making its mission a reality. An effective and compelling vision statement also allows the school to minimize actions and endeavors that might impact its ability to achieve its mission.

Successful PLC leaders are aware that mission and vision statements must be more than just words on paper. Instead, they need to guide actions and behaviors in the school on a daily basis. These statements document the shared beliefs and understandings that unite every individual and collaborative team within the school. They provide a blueprint for improvement and must therefore underpin the shared commitments enacted by all.

In the early stages of the PLC transformation, structures must be established to ensure that adequate time and input is allowed for the shared development of mission and vision statements. School leaders need to consider how they are going to create the forums, time, and processes necessary to allow representatives of the school to jointly develop a common understanding of the direction in which the school aims to go. The following are some key points to consider when devising structures to support the development of mission and vision statements.

- Educators who are expected to contribute significantly to the PLC process must receive the opportunity for input, discussion, and debate. This ensures that there is a strong sense of ownership in and commitment to the direction set. As the mission and vision expressed in the statements must be lived by all community members, particularly the educators doing the work on a daily basis, structures established to develop the school's direction must allow time for the development of a compelling argument as to why everyone should commit to the PLC process.

- Participants involved in devising the direction outlined in the school's mission and vision statements must be informed and knowledgeable. If a diverse range of stakeholders is to be involved, school leaders must invest in building their capacity to contribute. This will help to ensure that the future direction developed for the school is research based, credible, and focused on improving standards of student learning.

- The structures established must allow time for deep and meaningful discussions to take place. Rushed or poorly planned meetings prevent a solid foundation from being laid, which can jeopardize possible future action. Prior preparation, adequate resourcing, and a clear procedure will ensure that this foundational undertaking is as efficient as possible.

- The school's mission and vision should challenge old paradigms, not reinforce them. The development of mission and vision statements provides the opportunity to test the shared beliefs of educators and key stakeholders, so the structures established must allow for beliefs to be tested and challenged, particularly in relation to the ability of all students to learn at high levels.

- To turn the school's mission and vision into meaningful action, school leaders must ensure that the community connects with and internalizes it. Every meeting and every communication strategy should in some way be used as an opportunity to further cement the school's mission and vision into every school community member's consciousness.

- The school leadership team needs to be mindful that as the school becomes increasingly effective as a PLC, and as educators' skills and capabilities develop, mission and vision statements may need to be revised due to the increased collective understanding of what the school can achieve by working as a PLC. For example, when starting the PLC journey, educators might not be convinced of the impact they can have on student learning and may therefore limit the vision they set. As they start seeing the results of working in collaborative teams, their understanding of the level of learning possible will rise. In this case, the school's mission and vision may need to be reviewed in light of the increasing levels of student achievement.

To understand the importance of ongoing attention to the school's mission and vision, consider the following comparison of two schools that differ significantly in their approach to the structural implementation of their mission and vision statements.

> Several years ago, the staff and community at Northwest School put a lot of work into developing the school's mission and vision statements. At this time, the leadership team formed focus groups of staff members and worked with key stakeholders to develop a well-articulated document that encapsulated
>
> *continued* →

the ethos that the school was trying to achieve. Everyone involved in the process was happy with the developed document, and they celebrated its completion. The school proudly displayed its vision and mission in the school foyer and they also appeared as a footer in the fortnightly school newsletter.

Over the years, however, the school's mission and vision have become less prominent in the minds of the educators and other community members as they focus instead on the daily tasks they have to perform. When a school leader speaks to a member of staff who joined the school after the mission and vision were developed, she is shocked to discover that this teacher is unaware of the school's strategic direction. When she quizzes longer-serving staff members, she discovers that they also have only a superficial understanding of the school's mission and vision. She realizes that these important cornerstones of the school have never performed their intended role of underpinning and guiding the daily work of the school community. Instead, they have become at best another accountability task for educators to tick off their to-do list—and at worst, they have been forgotten altogether.

At Southeast School, the situation is quite different. Although both schools went through a similar process to devise their mission and vision statements, the school leaders at Southeast also developed a plan to ensure that the mission and vision would be lived at the school on a daily basis. Rather than simply adding the mission of the school to the often-ignored footer of the newsletter, articles in the newsletter regularly refer to the mission; further, it features prominently on the school's website and is repeatedly presented to parents at all school-based events. Meanwhile, teachers in their classrooms link the school's mission to the learning goals they share with students.

To ensure that teachers keep the school's mission and vision at the forefront of their practice, each staff meeting begins with reference to the statements, and short activities are organized for each meeting to ensure that educators are internalizing the mission and vision. Staff even generate ideas through addressing the question, What can staff do to show that they are living the school's mission and vision? These ideas for professional behaviors are constantly discussed. It is expected that all teachers will demonstrate them. Staff are regularly encouraged to assess their actions and professional practice against the statements and discard practices and programs that do not directly contribute toward their achievement. Even small gains are acknowledged, while milestones are cause for community celebration.

At Southeast School, the mission and vision statements are no longer words on a piece of long-forgotten paper. Instead, they have become so institutionalized that they are the driving force behind the school's culture supported by the structures purposely put in place.

## STRUCTURES THAT PROMOTE DISTRIBUTED LEADERSHIP

Becoming a PLC necessitates changes to the leadership structures of the school. In a PLC, each collaborative team is empowered to undertake collective inquiry to achieve the PLC mission of high levels of learning for all students. Working together, educators become co-learners as they reflect on learning data to improve teaching practices. This change in the basic dynamic of the way in which educators work means that leadership is no longer centralized but instead distributed across the school. In this way, professional collaboration is a foundation for *distributed leadership*.

Distributed leadership concentrates on collaborative interaction among individuals in formal and informal leadership roles, sharing out some of the leadership and management responsibilities while keeping the leadership team at the center (Dinham, 2008; Harris & Spillane, 2008). Harris (2014) describes distributed leaders as being:

> primarily concerned with mobilizing leadership experience at all levels in the organization to generate more opportunities for change and to generate the capacity for improvement. The emphasis is upon *interdependent interaction and practice* rather than *individual and independent actions* associated with those with formal leadership roles and responsibilities. (p. 36)

Harris (2014) emphasizes that distributed leadership is about connecting leadership practice as closely as possible to learning and teaching practices and empowering others as partners in school transformation. Distributed leadership therefore addresses Fullan's (2011) assertion that there has been an over-reliance on the "wrong drivers" for system reform in which external accountability is presumed to drive results. Leadership in a PLC empowers people to perform by building their capacity to do so and holds them accountable for performance (Sahlberg, 2011).

However, distributed leadership doesn't just happen. The distributed leadership approach of a highly effective PLC has to be carefully planned, and structures must be created to allow for it to develop. Development of educators' ability to thrive under a distributed leadership approach—and the opportunity to exercise these skills—needs to be deliberately structured into the school's operations and meeting schedules. Advancing the school's journey to become a high-performing PLC requires the establishment of planned opportunities to support the development of knowledge about how to work collaboratively together, how to deal with conflict as it arises, how to maintain a professional focus when drawing conclusions from student learning data, how to identify best teaching practices, and so on. The structuring of such opportunities as part of the school's operations provides a regular avenue for ongoing support and professional learning for collaborative team facilitators and members.

Leadership in a PLC is distributed to ensure that team members have a sense of ownership and a commitment to team actions. Without some overall coordination, however, the work can quickly deviate off track. Under the PLC model, the role of the principal and leadership team is to serve collaborative teams as they focus on achieving the school's mission—and part of this is the responsibility to grow leaders across the school. As such, it is essential that regular and targeted meetings are held between collaborative team facilitators and the leadership team with a focus on how best to lead a collaborative team.

Again, we turn to the example of two contrasting schools to demonstrate the way in which structures that promote distributed leadership are essential for PLC success.

The principal of Northwest School has recently attended a professional learning session on PLCs and is excited about what this transformation might bring. Educators at the school are already working in teams, and the principal feels sure that with a little refinement and some advice and professional reading, the teams will be able to quickly adjust their work to be more in line with the collaborative team practices that distinguish a PLC. When he approaches the school's existing team facilitators, they are eager to learn more about how to work collaboratively.

The principal meets with the facilitators and outlines the PLC process. He explains collaborative teamwork and gives the facilitators articles to read. Upon monitoring the first few team meetings, he is pleased with the transformation. He believes that each collaborative team should be given independence to do their work, so he gives each team increasing autonomy. Yet when he revisits the teams several months later, the principal is shocked to discover that many have reverted to their old way of working or have even stopped meeting altogether.

The principal of Southeast School attends the same professional learning session, but she approaches implementation differently. Upon her return to school, she first works with her leadership team to develop an implementation plan with the aim of making sure that the transformation is paced out as much as possible. The principal then conducts a whole-staff professional learning session in which staff critically consider how the PLC process will assist them to achieve higher levels of learning for all students. At this meeting, assumptions and beliefs are respectfully challenged and interest is generated.

The principal ensures that she and key members of her leadership team meet regularly with individual team facilitators to discuss how things are going and offer support in any way necessary. They identify common issues or concerns across teams, and these become the focus of professional learning for facilitators and team members. Existing forums, such as staff meetings, are used to enhance the capabilities of educators to work interdependently as part of a PLC. Besides their individual meetings with school leaders, team facilitators get together on a regular basis to share their teams' journeys, celebrate their successes, and learn from one another.

Professional learning about the PLC process is targeted to meet the needs of each team, and teams are encouraged to share best PLC practices. Not only do school leaders support and assist teams but they set aside and protect time to ensure that this happens. Because building the collaborative capabilities of educators is seen as a high priority by school leaders, it becomes embedded in the way the school operates. Continuous capability building fosters in educators a deep sense that they will be continually supported in the new way they are being asked to work.

## STRUCTURES FOR SCHOOLWIDE COMMUNICATION

Effective channels of communication are essential in any transformative process to ensure that all community members clearly understand the change. When establishing a PLC, it is vital that communication structures are reviewed and then modified, or dismantled and re-established, to eliminate boundaries and hierarchies that inhibit the flow of information.

Schools are complex organizations that involve a lot of daily administrative and organizational procedures. Communication of these procedures and their requirements can clog meeting agendas and collaborative team time, so it is vital that educators can access this necessary information in a way that does not involve valuable collaboration time being lost. Communication structures need to effectively manage the volume of information that educators need to know on a daily basis so that precious team time is not wasted on discussions of lower-impact issues.

School leaders can establish a range of communication structures and procedures so that such information is readily available to educators. Both written communication structures— such as daily bulletins, emails, published meeting minutes, and bulletin boards—and oral communication structures—daily staff briefings, time-bound information-sharing sessions at staff meetings, and informal direct conversations—assist greatly in ensuring ready access to necessary information.

Introducing and utilizing communication structures such as these also ensures that time at collaborative team meetings is reserved for purposeful dialogue and discussion about the primary purpose of school: student learning. Any communication structures established within a PLC must not intrude on the collaborative team mandate of productive dialogue on the issues that matter most in achieving high levels of learning for all students.

Developing efficient channels of communication that limit non-essential information will allow the communication landscape to shift in a way that privileges in-depth dialogue among educators about teaching practice and student learning. By ensuring that the required communication structures are in place to share important organizational and administrative requirements that schools must attend to, school leaders create opportunity and time to allow teams to get on with the task of improving student learning.

The following scenario highlights the markedly different outcomes that two different approaches to schoolwide communication can have.

At Northwest School, collaborative teams have been embedded into the school's operations for several years. All educators are allocated to a team and a schoolwide collaborative meeting schedule is established. School leaders are happy with the structures that have been put in place, but they have become increasingly concerned that there has been little improvement in student learning. Even the educators who were initially most enthusiastic about the PLC process have begun to exhibit higher levels of frustration, and some have complained publicly that collaborative team meetings intrude on time when they could be planning lessons or marking assessments.

The leadership team at Northwest School decides to question a few of the more dedicated educators to gather information about what is going on. Educator after educator reports that meetings are being consumed with the sharing of information, the completion of administrative duties, and other tasks not directly related to student learning. When the school leaders dig deeper to analyze the demands being placed on teams, they are shocked to discover that many are coming from the leadership team itself.

At Southeast School, by contrast, the leadership team takes steps to explicitly build consensus among staff about which tasks are appropriate to include on a collaborative team's meeting agenda. Educators learn how to "parking lot" some less-pressing issues when they arise during collaborative team discussions so that they can follow up at the appropriate time. A daily bulletin is established and becomes the central point for all school communications and reminders.

The leadership team models a focus on learning by acting as a filter to make sure that staff meetings focus on professional learning or collaborative problem solving. They monitor collaborative team meetings and respectfully challenge teams when items appear that do not relate to the PLC process. The leadership team raises the status and importance of collaborative team meetings by supporting teams to ensure that they can focus on the right work.

## STRUCTURES TO ENSURE EFFECTIVE COLLABORATIVE TEAMS

Most people involved in school improvement agree that the most critical factor is time. What's more, research validates this commonly held belief. According to education professor Mary Anne Raywid (1993), "Collaborative time for teachers to undertake and then sustain school improvement may be more important than equipment, facilities or even staff development."

Given that collaborative teams are the engines of school improvement when it comes to achieving high levels of student learning, one of the most important questions that needs to be resolved when transforming from a conventional school into a PLC is, When will collaborative teams actually meet? In a true PLC, the work of the collaborative team becomes so embedded in the daily efforts of educators that they see it as an integral part of the school's operations. As such, allocating adequate time for collaborative team meetings is an imperative consideration for schools on the journey toward becoming a PLC.

As discussed in action 4.2, the authority to modify the school's structures, timetable, or schedule typically rests with school leaders, so it is ultimately the leader or leadership team who will have the power to provide meeting time. However, even though they have the authority to alter the existing structures, leaders should still consult educators for their views on the options available. This approach is one way of distributing leadership beyond the leadership team as possible structural changes to meeting schedules are considered.

It is important that the time provided for collaborative teams to meet is not simply added to educators' already busy schedules. If the priority of the school is to improve student learning outcomes, and if collaboration between educators is seen as a crucial component in achieving this outcome, then adding another meeting outside of school hours sends the wrong message to educators about the value of collaborative team interactions. The time allocated for collaborative teams to meet needs to be during the working school day and should be built in to the weekly or biweekly meeting schedule of the school. It must be protected and given priority over all other school endeavors.

Beyond these basic principles, the specific answer to the question, When will collaborative teams meet? will be as varied as the schools themselves. Each school needs to answer this question in light of its current context and reality. While the solutions will vary from school to school, a time must be found. As challenging as the search for time can be, there are many creative ways to resolve this issue. Structural changes that school leaders we've worked with have made to find this time include the following.

- Repurposing an existing meeting time
- Using student assembly times
- Aligning educators' preparation and planning times
- Adjusting the start or end of the school day

- Combining classes involved in non-instructional activities to free up teachers to meet collaboratively
- Banking time by adjusting learning session length

By providing team meeting time during the working school day, school leaders send a strong message that collaborative team time is key when it comes to the PLC goal of improving student learning outcomes.

Making and finding time is a necessary structural consideration when beginning the journey to become a PLC, but how that time is used is also critical. While scheduling time for collaborative teams to meet is vital, it does not necessarily mean that the allocated time will be used productively to impact teacher practice or student learning. Educators can become frustrated and begin to see this time as yet another obligation that keeps them from getting things done. Realizing the potential of collaborative team meetings requires that all team members have both the drive and the skills necessary to transform these meetings into dynamic learning forums where the school's PLC mission and vision come to life. Collaborative team meetings are the primary opportunities for teachers to work together, so these meetings must be reserved for in-depth professional discussions about the learning program, student learning data, and most effective teaching practices in improving student learning.

Given the need to ensure that collaborative team meetings remain focused on the most critical issues related to teaching and learning, school leaders should consider and, where possible, implement school structures to support the completion of necessary tasks that arise from these discussions. Aligned planning time, when educators have synchronized release time from teaching responsibilities, is one way to ensure that teams of educators can carry out the organizational tasks that flow on from decisions and commitments agreed on at collaborative team meetings. These tasks could include more detailed planning of the learning program, continued work on common formative assessment tasks, processing of data, planning for intervention sessions, and so on.

The provision of additional time will depend on many factors, including the size of the school, the number of teachers at each grade level, industrial agreements, and the resources available to the school. While the success of a school's transformation into a PLC is not dependent on this extra time, it is one way to ensure planning and organizational tasks do not intrude into collaborative team meeting time.

Consider the following scenario, which compares how two schools deal with the issue of structuring collaborative team time.

> At Northwest School, the school leaders decide that collaborative teams will meet weekly after school for one hour. Teams are told their meeting time and given no opportunity to query it. From the onset, educators are vocal in their negativity toward the meeting time, with the result that they meet

because of compliance rather than a sense of the importance of the work. Most educators see collaborative team meetings as something extra that they are required to do, rather than as a practice essential to their endeavors to achieve high levels of learning for all.

At Southeast School, the school leaders review all the meeting arrangements that have developed in the school over time. They work from the premise that if the work is important, it is important that they find time for teachers to meet during the contractual school day. The leaders decide that they will not negotiate about the fact that collaborative teams must meet for an hour each week, but they are flexible on when this meeting occurs.

The school leaders consider a range of ways to create time for collaborative team meetings, including repurposing existing meeting times, aligning common planning time, providing additional resources, and creatively using assembly time. Once they have a few options they think are feasible, they ask staff to suggest any other options they can come up with and then have them list the advantages and disadvantages of each suggestion.

Once educators are involved in this way, a preferred option surfaces, and the school leaders take the necessary steps to ensure that this time becomes the protected meeting time for each collaborative team. Following their involvement in the process of establishing the meeting time, school staff members are enthusiastic about how they can use this time to achieve high levels of learning for all students.

## STRUCTURES THAT FOSTER COLLABORATION

A collaborative team without common purpose functions more as a group than as a team. To mitigate this issue, collaborative teams are often structured according to commonalities among teachers. In primary schools, teams are usually formed based on the common content that teachers deliver to their students, while in secondary schools, teams may be made up of educators who all teach the same grade level or subject area. These commonalities allow team members to work together to achieve a common goal.

Since the primary approach that collaborative teams use is one of collective inquiry, in which teams identify and address issues relevant to their students' learning, the most important consideration when educators come together to form a team is to identify the team goals that will unite them in their work. The more specific and targeted the goal, the stronger the bonds that unite the team. For example, in a primary school setting, all the teachers of grade 4 students may form a collaborative team. United by the common skills and knowledge they have identified that all grade 4 students need to master, the team might come up with a goal: By the end of the third nine weeks, 80 percent of students will score proficient (90 percent) or above on the skills and knowledge related to grade 4 prioritized standards for the topic of fractions, as evidenced by a common assessment to be administered on March 3. This goal instantly unites the educators because it compels them to work both individually and interdependently to achieve their aim. If all educators don't work toward achieving the goal in their individual classrooms, the chance that the collective goal will be met is minimal. Carefully considering the goals that individual educators have in common and constructing collaborative teams based on these common goals provides a solid platform for future endeavors and inquiry.

Once collaborative teams have been established, it is vital that school leaders consider the ongoing support that teams need to be able to work collaboratively. As noted in chapter 3 (page 35), just placing educators in a team, even one that shares strong interdependent goals, doesn't mean that each individual team member will have the skills required to work collaboratively. Team members will need to be skilled at making sure that conversations focus on achievement of agreed-on goals and remain respectful, constructive, and objective. Without professional learning to foster the skills required for collaborative interaction, teams can become unproductive and negative. As such, PLCs must develop structures that support ongoing development of the skills and strategies necessary for collaborative team members to work effectively together. For example, teams will need to learn how to develop norms in a range of areas. Other examples include the following.

- How to develop reasonable but challenging goals that focus on student learning
- How to construct rigorous and reliable common formative assessments
- Ways to develop and strengthen team trust
- How to reach agreement
- How to discuss and interpret learning data
- How to communicate effectively

While educators will quickly discover the need to increase their knowledge and understanding in these areas as they begin to work as a collaborative team, their lack of knowledge should not be an excuse to delay the start of the PLC journey. These issues will naturally arise as collaborative teams do the work, providing a compelling purpose for professional learning in these areas. Directed and specific professional learning on how to work effectively as a team increases the ability of the team to get on with the real work that they are meeting about—the learning of the students they serve. When equipped with the skills to work effectively as a team, educators gain professional confidence and improve their ability to ensure high levels of learning for all students.

The following scenario demonstrates the importance of professional learning designed to foster collaboration.

At Northwest School, collaborative teams have been established and time to meet has been arranged. The collaborative teams have developed norms that outline the professional behaviors expected during team meetings. Team members have a clear understanding of the PLC process and are enthusiastic about the work they will be doing together. The teams identify the elements of the curriculum that they want students to be proficient in during the next cycle of learning, collaboratively develop common assessments, and hold discussions about the learning data collected to identify student learning progress.

All these developments seem positive, but when a member of Northwest's leadership team sits in on a collaborative team meeting, she is shocked to discover that the team just seems to be going through the motions. Discussions about the learning data are shallow, cordial, and brief, with very few opposing points of view being aired and debated, and the leader notes that the team struggles to develop quality common assessments. By the end of the meeting, even the school leader is confused about which actions the team members have agreed to implement before the next meeting.

At Southeast School, the leadership team looks carefully at the agenda of its staff meeting and realizes that the majority of the time is spent on items that don't have a high impact on student learning. Realizing that collaborative team members often need to develop new skills and capabilities to be successful, the leaders strip the staff meeting agenda of these low-priority items and restructure this time for professional learning designed to develop the skills and aptitudes team members will require to get better at working as a high-functioning collaborative team.

The leaders monitor each team, and when common struggles are evident, all the members of that team participate in professional learning at the next staff meeting. Teams that are making headway or have overcome an issue are invited to present. At the end of these meetings, the educators are questioned about what else they need to know or be able to do to support the work of their collaborative team. Because collaborative teams receive regular and targeted professional learning in this way, team morale at Southeast is strong, and the collaborative functioning of teams quickly begins to improve.

## DATA-PROCESSING STRUCTURES

The main purpose of collaborative team meetings is to provide the forum for educators to be involved in highly effective, job-embedded action research in which they investigate the teaching and learning process. Based on the available learning data, educators in a team should select a specific aspect of student learning to examine in order to first gain insight into what is happening in their classrooms and then identify the most effective teaching practices to implement. Collaborative teams in a PLC use learning data to establish goals, provide evidence of effective teaching, and monitor progress to enhance individual and collective teaching practice. Through the effective analysis of learning data, collaborative teams develop the capacity to manage their own improvement as they engage in job-embedded professional learning. As such, the analysis of data is an integral component of the work of collaborative teams and the PLC process.

The establishment of school structures to manage the processing and collation of data embeds the process of collective inquiry in the culture of the school. Without this support, valuable team time will be devoted to the collation of data rather than to discussions of how teacher practice can improve student achievement. Organized systems to collate and represent data before collaborative teams discuss and analyze them must be established at the school level so that teams can dedicate their time directly to the achievement of higher levels of learning for students. One possible option is the establishment of data-processing teams made up of existing administrative or nonteaching personnel whose role is to manage and disseminate data in a timely and effective manner.

The following scenario compares two contrasting schools to demonstrate the impact that data-processing structures can have on the functioning of collaborative teams.

> The principal of Northwest School is pleased with the way teachers have adapted to the PLC approach. Team members work collaboratively and understand the components of the PLC process. However, collaborative teams constantly report that they don't have enough time at meetings to undertake rich and rigorous discussions about best teaching practice as revealed by student learning data.
>
> Upon further investigation, the leadership team finds that much meeting time is spent perusing students' responses to common assessments and collating data. Collaborative team members are focused and busy as they crunch numbers on calculators and work out percentages to reveal how close they are to the targets they have set. However, what little discussion there is centers on numbers rather than the team's analysis of the data. By the time the meeting ends, school leaders can sense the frustration as many overdue agenda items are once again carried over to the next meeting.
>
> At Southeast School, school leaders understand clearly that the primary purpose of the learning data collected by collaborative teams is to provide evidence of student learning, allowing the team to have discussions about the collective actions they will take based on the data. They also understand that teams need to access the learning data in a timely manner so that they can immediately adjust their response to ensure that students who are struggling or excelling have their specific learning needs met.

As such, the school leaders systematically and regularly review the ways that collaborative teams are using and collating data. Based on this knowledge, and in cooperation with collaborative team facilitators, the leaders investigate the best system to process and collate the data. As teams become more data driven and responsive, the leaders ensure that they are establishing a whole-school approach to data collation. Data-entry spreadsheets are created that can be quickly modified by teams to work with each new common assessment developed. Formulas and conditional formatting of cells are developed to automate as much of the data calculation as possible. When educators lack skill in the program they are using, they receive professional development. Over a period of time, a system is developed that allows educators to enter their data quickly in advance of the team meeting and bring the collated data back to the team for discussion. The collaborative team time and discussions now focus more on analyzing and acting on the data, since precious meeting time is not consumed with processing the data.

Southeast's school leaders constantly check with teams to ensure that the system suits their needs. A process of continuous improvement is established as agreed-on adjustments are made to ensure that each team has the ability to turn data into specific information and action.

## DECISION-MAKING STRUCTURES

Hattie (2009) concludes that the most powerful strategy for guaranteeing that students learn at high levels is to ensure that teachers work collaboratively to identify essential learnings, gather evidence of student learning through ongoing assessments, and then use the evidence of learning to discuss, evaluate, and plan for continued student learning. This model requires educators to make collaborative decisions and take action based on the evidence of student learning.

The inquiry process demands that leaders grant each team the authority and responsibility to solve problems of practice in creative, innovative, and evidence-backed ways. Naturally, the school's mission and vision must guide the approaches implemented, but school leaders need to ensure that school structures enable collaborative teams to make their own decisions in alignment with the school's strategic direction. Collaborative teams need the opportunity to experiment and take risks as they inquire into various ways to improve student learning. As long as the data provide confirmation that the action the team is taking is having a positive impact, school leaders need to let go of the notion that school improvement and improved student learning are only possible through the decisions they make.

The creation of structures that shift decision-making responsibilities to teachers enables everyone to contribute toward the goal of high levels of learning for all students. However, it does not absolve school leaders from responsibility for school improvement. In a PLC, their role is to ensure that the goals that collaborative teams set are being achieved and to support collaborative teams by providing time and resources.

As a result of the reciprocal accountability this arrangement demands, school personnel are united as they work toward the achievement of the school mission and vision. Consider the following scenario featuring two PLC schools.

> The leaders of Northwest School have gained strong staff support for the implementation of the PLC process. They have conducted professional learning and developed an action plan.
>
> One school leader implements an accountability system to ensure that the leadership team is clear about what each team is up to and whether it is following the strategic direction that had been set. The leader requests that each team send her a list of the team's proposed actions after each meeting. The leader will then check the actions, and if she agrees they will have a positive impact on improving student learning, she will communicate with the team and allow them to implement the proposed actions.
>
> After several months, the school leader notices that, while teams seem to be busy, there appears to be very little change in how teachers are teaching in their classrooms. In fact, even the actions that are approved seem to be implemented with little enthusiasm or genuine interest.
>
> At Southeast School, all staff understand that the purpose of the PLC process is to allow teams to inquire and make decisions about effective teaching practice to improve student learning. As such, the school leaders have made sure that all staff are involved in developing the school's mission and vision statements. These statements are constantly discussed in school forums, and over time they become entrenched in the culture of the school.
>
> With the knowledge that everyone on staff has a clear understanding of the direction of the school, the school leaders encourage teams to be as innovative as possible as they develop actions based on learning data. Teams understand that they have license to set their own course of action, so long as it is based on evidence of improved student learning and contributes to the achievement of the school mission and vision.
>
> The school leader remains informed on the actions and decisions teams are making but allows them to act autonomously. She knows that teams will review any decision they make in light of the data they receive and will quickly revise or abandon the action if it doesn't improve student learning. As a result, teams feel empowered, trusted, and supported as they work together.

## ADMINISTRATIVE STRUCTURES

We have already established that as collaborative teams begin to focus on the inquiry process and actively research best teaching practices, it is vital they are not diverted from this work by the less important tasks that can clog collaborative meeting agendas. The transformation from conventional school to PLC requires educators to work in different ways and on tasks that may not have been a priority in the past. In the initial stages of the PLC journey, the tendency of teams will be to default to previous ways of working and familiar tasks. For example, discussions about the organization of an upcoming excursion—while important— are much easier and more familiar to newly formed collaborative teams than discussions aimed at analyzing learning data to identify the best teaching practices.

School leaders need to ensure that they are putting school structures in place to reduce or minimize the administrative and technical tasks that can often intrude into valuable collaborative team meeting time. While these tasks are important for school operations and can't be eliminated entirely, school leaders need to review existing school structures and free educators of as many of these second-tier tasks as possible. As previously discussed, organizational arrangements will vary from school to school depending on their unique circumstances. It is vital, however, if we are asking educators to work in different ways and on different work than they are used to, that we give due consideration to removing some of the traditional tasks educators have been required to perform. Ultimately, collaborative teamwork is doomed to failure if school leaders do not find ways to reduce the number of tasks educators perform that could distract from the PLC purpose of improving student learning.

By ensuring that administrative or technical tasks are dealt with by others, addressed in other forums, or quarantined to a brief, specific time on the collaborative team meeting agenda, school leaders show that they actively support the important work of collaborative teams aimed at ensuring high levels of learning for all students.

At Northwest School, the leadership team comes back from a PLC session excited for the school to commence its journey toward becoming a PLC. School staff members are always eager to try new things, and they are quickly convinced of the benefits for student learning. They particularly like the fact that time will be created for them to collaborate with a focus on improving student learning—the very reason most of them entered the profession in the first place.

The PLC process start off well, but after only a few weeks, the school leaders begin to notice that staff seem to be increasingly tired and run down. When school leaders try to speak to one of their most trusted members of staff about the situations, she explains that she doesn't really have time to talk because she just has too much to do: "We just don't seem to ever get on top

*continued* ➜

of things. We're working hard on this PLC stuff, but we still have everything else to do as well."

At Southeast School, school leaders understand that any change process can be time consuming and energy draining if not handled in the right way. The leaders know that educators will become overburdened if they are asked to adopt new practices while keeping up all the other tasks for which they have previously been responsible. As such, when the idea of working to become a PLC meets with the support of the majority of staff, the leadership team decides to assess which existing practices and approaches they can abandon or at least modify to ease the pressure on educators. They use the opportunity to show staff that it is OK to abandon ineffective practices if they impact the school's ability to achieve its mission and vision.

## STRUCTURES THAT MAXIMIZE STUDENT LEARNING

As educators start to adopt the belief that all students can learn at high levels, they will quickly realize that differentiated levels of support and varying amounts of time are necessary to ensure that all students reach this goal. Some students will need extra support and time to reach the required standard of learning, while others will already have achieved the desired level before direct teaching of skills and knowledge even commences, complicating the task of catering to the learning needs of all students.

Leaders can address the need for differentiation by introducing intervention sessions into the school's schedule. Providing time for intervention sessions is a key element of the way that PLCs operate. While experience has shown that intervention is not the most immediate consideration for schools commencing the PLC journey, it is an issue that will arise as educators pursue the goal of achieving high levels of learning for all students. Schools cannot claim to be operating as PLCs until they have developed timely, systematic, and directive interventions.

The process that PLCs use to provide additional time and support to students is often referred to as response to intervention (RTI). RTI experts Tom Hierck and Chris Weber (2014) suggest that RTI is best understood as the practices and processes that represent the proactive efforts of educators to ensure that students receive the support they need as soon as they show signs of needing it. RTI is the mechanism for providing timely, targeted, and research-based interventions until the barriers to learning are overcome.

The way that RTI sessions are incorporated into the school's existing structures and time-tables will require careful thought and consideration by school leaders. Chris Weber and Nathan Lang-Raad (2015) warn that educators become overwhelmed by the complexities of what the RTI system might look like, causing them to struggle to embed the principles and practices of intervention with success. The goal of the school leader in a PLC should be to ensure that the systems of support don't become complicated by complex rules, rigid structures, and laborious paperwork.

As part of the restructuring of their school, school leaders may find it beneficial to consider their RTI interventions in terms of a three-tier system of support (Buffum, Mattos, & Malone, 2018).

- **TIER 1** of the RTI system involves the design of focused and rigorous units of instruction. Educators use formative assessment tasks to build engaging, differentiated pathways to ensure that students achieve at the required standard. Tier 1 occurs within the normal classroom program offered by teachers. Interventions at this tier include the strategies and approaches teachers use to group students based on learning needs, the focus teacher groups they establish in each content area, and the ways they structure time and support into their teaching program.

- **TIER 2** intervention sessions normally occur at specific times during the week when the regular teaching program temporarily pauses to allow students additional time and support to master important skills and knowledge recently covered in class. Students requiring Tier 2 intervention are identified by the team's assessment practices. Tier 2 intervention sessions also allow students who have mastered the required skills and knowledge to consolidate these skills and apply them in new ways.

  Teachers usually provide Tier 2 interventions to small groups of students; ideally the collaborative team member with the strongest teaching practice in this area would provide the intervention. For these students, the goal of Tier 2 intervention is mastery of prioritized course content at the required grade-level standard. Students achieving at or above the required standard may learn in larger groups and engage in tasks that enrich, extend, or require them to apply their new knowledge in some way.

- **TIER 3** intervention sessions targeted those students who are significantly struggling in key areas of the curriculum. These students are typically multiple grade levels behind their peers in fundamental skills. Tier 3 sessions are built into the schedules of just the students who need intensive assistance to achieve at the appropriate level. Educators must ensure that they are providing this level of assistance without taking students away from grade-level coursework at Tier 1 (Buffum et al., 2018). Interventions at this level are adjusted to meet the specific learning needs of each student until that student adequately responds to the interventions. The system of RTI support heightens in intensity between Tier 2 and Tier 3, becoming more intensive by increasing the time of the intervention and decreasing the student-to-student ratio.

By scheduling Tier 2 and Tier 3 sessions into the school's timetable, school leaders assist teachers to overcome one of the major challenges that arises in making high levels of learning a reality for their students in a PLC. While schools will find different ways to structure the opportunity for Tier 2 and Tier 3 interventions, practice has revealed some common threads that can help school leaders consider the options available to them. If collaborative teams are going to be able to operate effectively, school leaders must ensure that they have created the opportunity for students to receive RTI support during the normal school day. This will involve close examination of the school's master schedule in order to embed intervention sessions into the daily operations of the school. Many schools find that the most efficient way to ensure the inclusion of intervention sessions on the school's master schedule is to build the master timetable around intervention sessions, while other schools have found merit in staggering intervention sessions across the school day so that the use of additional personnel can be maximized. Intervention is a key structural consideration in the journey to become a PLC, and whole-school solutions ensure that it is seen as a priority and built systematically across the school.

When we work with school leaders who are considering structures to support intervention, they often ask us how long and how frequent Tier 2 and Tier 3 intervention sessions should be. The simple answer is that they should be as long as they need to be—and not a second longer. This is because the time for Tier 2 intervention sessions is taken from teachers' regular teaching schedule. Many schools have found that a half-hour block reserved four times a week is a satisfactory compromise.

The following scenario compares two PLC schools as they work to implement the multileveled RTI approach to intervention.

At Northwest School, the staff have embraced the PLC philosophy and approach it with rigor and determination. They have established suitable meeting times, developed strong norms, and are highly skilled in the components of the PLC approach. The school leaders notice that teaching practice in classrooms is changing and that teachers are much clearer on which practices they should implement in different circumstances with different students.

However, although there have been some gains in student learning, they haven't been as significant as expected. Teachers are beginning to become discouraged, both by the poor progress of some students and by their inability to cater to students who developed proficiency early in the learning cycle. They also complain that struggling students are constantly being taken out of class during core instruction time and are thus falling even further behind.

At Southeast School, the leaders understand that no matter how good the efforts of educators, some students will require a different amount of time and support to enable them to reach the required standard. As such, the school leaders have built a schoolwide RTI system that provides differentiated amounts of support and time for those students who need it. The system is coordinated across the school, and the leadership team have made sure all educators are clear on how it works. Teachers are also involved in reviewing the system so that it is continuously improved. Specific intervention times are delineated on the school's master timetable, thus solving the problem of students missing core instruction time.

As a result of these actions, teachers feel that a safety net exists that will allow struggling students to receive the support they need, while students who have reached proficiency will be able to have their learning further enriched. The school leaders have ensured that the focus of the school is truly on learning rather than just the delivery of content.

## STRUCTURES FOR CELEBRATING PLC PROGRESS

Transforming a school into a PLC is a significant process that involves continuous change. As such, it can be a relentless and tiring undertaking in which staff can become exhausted and enthusiasm can wane. Celebrations, both small and large, are vital to ensure that educators have the energy and momentum to keep doing the work they are being asked to do. Celebrations that recognize and support positive achievements remind members of the learning community that the school is serious about achieving the goals that it has set.

Every change process has distinct transition points. The celebration of significant milestones and smaller *inch pebbles* helps to re-energize teams and promote continued progress toward the achievement of the school's mission and vision. In a PLC, educators are asked to become more accountable for their results, and celebrations provide a way to publicly recognize incremental progress. They also create important opportunities to connect a given change to its purpose in moving the school toward the goal of high-level learning for all.

While celebration should be everyone's responsibility within a PLC, it is the role of the school leaders to ensure that structures are in place to make celebrations a regular part of the school's operations. School leaders make collaborative teams comfortable with celebrations when they consciously schedule celebration time into school meetings, build structures to acknowledge positive steps forward, and publicly recognize and celebrate success. Celebration can take place in a range of forums, including at meetings and assemblies or through newsletters and school websites.

Ensuring that opportunities to celebrate are structured into the school's operations creates a culture of celebration that is itself a sign of the shifts that occur when the school transforms into a PLC. Celebrations not only foster cultural shift, they are an integral part of shifting the culture, as the following scenario illustrates.

The leadership team at Northwest School is extremely pleased with the way that the PLC journey has been going. Initial uptake has been slow, but after a period of regular reflection and continued capacity building, collaborative teams seem to be energized, engaged, and enjoying the process.

Yet after several months, the school leaders begin to get the sense that teams have regressed. Educators seem to be defaulting to their previous work habits,

*continued* ➙

or they have allowed the PLC process to morph into something else. They appear to be dispirited and disheartened. Fearing that educators might not believe that the PLC process will enhance student learning, one leader undertakes a fact-finding mission. Upon talking to educators, he gets the impression that they feel their efforts on behalf of students are unappreciated.

At Southeast School, the leadership team has adopted a distributed leadership approach to empower teams to search for their own solutions and determine their own actions as they work to achieve the school's mission and vision. Members of the leadership team review the goals that teams set and make sure that there is always acknowledgment when they make progress.

Where possible, school leaders personally and often publicly recognize educators whose practice is having the greatest impact on student learning. They ensure that they are exploiting every opportunity to celebrate growth in student learning. Time is set aside in each staff meeting to reflect on individual and team successes, and a formal team celebration highlighting improvements in the learning data is incorporated as part of the school's end-of-year staff meeting. Because the leadership team understands that continuous school improvement is hard and exhausting, they deliberately develop a school culture in which they acknowledge and celebrate any improved student learning outcome, no matter how small.

# REFLECTION

Leaders of PLCs need to develop a robust understanding of how structural and organizational arrangements interact with the cultural aspects in a PLC to enable them to respond effectively as issues arise. Leaders do not have to solve these issues themselves, but they do need to understand intimately the culture and structures within their school so that these can be modified should the need arise.

Changing structures in itself won't necessarily change schools. While there are common structural considerations that must be addressed during the PLC process, the specific actions required at each school will depend on the culture and structures that already exist. Some of these structures may be so firmly entrenched that undoing or modifying them will require deliberate action by school leaders. The challenge for leaders in a PLC is to ensure that they respond to the organic way in which the PLC process develops in their school by creating, monitoring, and adjusting structural arrangements that support and strengthen school improvement. Through the provision of structures that address the needs of the school community as they arise, the PLC will blossom.

# REFLECTIVE QUESTIONS: COMMITMENT 4—SHAPE SCHOOL STRUCTURES FOR SUCCESS

As you consider each reflective question, contemplate your response and identify the evidence that supports your thinking.

## ACTION 4.1: CONNECT STRUCTURES AND CULTURE

- How supportive are the structures of your school in relation to the mission of achieving high levels of learning for all students?

- How might you leverage the symbiotic relationship between school culture and structures to ensure the success of your school in becoming a PLC?

## ACTION 4.2: CHANGE STRUCTURES THROUGH SCHOOL LEADERSHIP

- What structures have school leaders put in place at your school to support teachers working collaboratively to improve student learning?

- In what ways do you or your leadership team monitor the structures established to ensure that they increase student learning success?

- What evidence do you have that the structures established have supported an increase in student learning?

## ACTION 4.3: CULTIVATE STRUCTURES FOR A HIGH-PERFORMING PLC

- Which of the structures outlined in this chapter have been implemented in your school? Which ones need further modification or development?

- What structures have been established to allow school staff to contribute to and develop a clear understanding of your school's mission and vision?

- In what ways have the school leaders at your school built the capacity for distributed leadership within collaborative teams?

- In what ways have leaders at your school ensured that collaborative team meetings aren't subverted by administrative tasks and other issues unrelated to student learning?

- To what extent has your school established structures for celebration and recognition of milestones both large and small?

# INSIGHTS FROM THE FIELD

*Our school has structured intervention blocks into the school day. Each team is now using these blocks of time to more effectively target the specific learning needs of our students.*

*When we organize our school timetable, we give intervention sessions the highest priority because we see them as essential to ensuring the provision of extra time and support for students who require it. Everything else is slotted in around intervention sessions.*

*As a leadership team, we recognize and celebrate the achievements of our teams. We've done the big celebration date with data night at the end of the year, when each team comes up and celebrates with the rest of the school. What we are now trying to encourage, and it's happening, is people are starting to celebrate just in their collaborative teams—so there's a lot more celebration.*

—IVY, ASSISTANT PRINCIPAL

*We mix up the teams with specialist teachers and representation from various grade levels so that everyone has input, and there are often really open and challenging discussions.*

*As a specialist, I feel very strongly that sometimes you can be treated as a bit of an island because of the nature of the job. But in our school, they have actively included all specialists as part of the PLC and as part of a collaborative team. I actually work in a block on Monday morning with grade 5–6 teachers, and I am a part of their team. I used to give time release for the rest of the teachers to access the PLC meeting times, so of course I couldn't attend the meetings myself—but the team said, "We want you there," and they changed their meeting time to after school in order to suit my needs. That's been really powerful because I'm informed; I'm there looking at the data; I know the children I'm working with. I find that the better informed we are about each child's needs, the better equipped we are to intervene or enrich their learning.*

*All the specialists are attached to a level and they are very much part of that team. We've also extended that. All the staff in the office are all now working one on one with children who've been deemed to need extra support. They'll listen to them read; it's making them feel part of the team. We also have a number of volunteers who come in, and we utilize them as well.*

—KAREN, SPECIALIST TEACHER

*We introduced intervention blocks twelve months ago, and now they're in every level. At the start, the teachers were saying, "We can't possibly timetable all of these." There were all these reasons why it couldn't happen. Whereas now, the teachers are saying, "We need more intervention blocks, and we need more team support."*

—DREW, PRINCIPAL

*Since we started the PLC journey, our pacing guide has become much more focused on the professional learning that is required to support our collaborative teams. We've got every meeting for the year on our calendar, and we adjust what's going to be addressed in each meeting depending on the needs of staff at the time. We start off with an overall view of where we need to get to, but we've already adjusted bits of the pacing guide to reflect what the teachers need to do to meet student needs.*

*Celebration is important for the students as well as teachers. We celebrate their achievements. The teachers are feeding back their data to the students as well. I'm going to assembly now knowing that every single award I'm about to give out will be related to learning, it will be about a specific learning goal the kids have achieved.*

—CHRIS, PRINCIPAL

*We've done staff meeting celebrations. The other night was an example. We got teams to present their data, and we really celebrated where we were at with the journey. It's very much become part of our review process. Everything we're doing as a PLC is talked about, reviewed, and celebrated.*

—AMELIA, ASSISTANT PRINCIPAL

# CHAPTER 5
# Create Clarity in Collaboration

*A lack of clarity could put the brakes on any journey to success.*

—Steve Maraboli

Every day, students behave in ways that will impact their learning. Every day, educators make decisions that will affect their teaching. And every day, leaders in schools act in ways that will influence their staff's practices, motivations, and attitudes. What we don't often scrutinize in these seemingly effortless decisions is why some behaviors are successful and why others are not.

Our experience has taught us that while many factors impact success, it is essential to understand what you want to achieve, the steps required to achieve it, and the ways you will monitor when you have achieved it. It is through this clarity that educators can develop powerful behaviors.

PLCs engage in a relentless pursuit to understand, with clarity, what impacts their core business of learning. Clarity helps all stakeholders in schools build the culture and structures required to ensure that all learning is at high levels. We've already discussed the importance of aligning culture and structures in this book (see chapter 4, page 55), but cultural and structural changes will not improve results unless all stakeholders know exactly—that is, with precision and clarity—what and how they will go about achieving goals that are related to the culture they are trying to achieve. Commitment 5 focuses specifically on how school leaders can harness the power of clarity to both create and communicate the cultural and structural changes that are required to ensure that the PLC transformation is a systematic and ongoing process of school improvement.

Clarity for the transformational leader in a PLC is as important as the windows and mirrors on a car. These features allow us to see what's approaching, what's around us, and where we've already been. By being clear on what is coming up, understanding the current reality, and reflecting on the journey so far, a PLC leader is empowered to take the actions required to arrive at the destination of high levels of learning for all students.

# KEY ACTIONS

To explain commitment 5, we will outline three key actions leaders require to ensure they create clarity in their school's transformation to a PLC.

- **ACTION 5.1:** Create clarity for shared understanding.
- **ACTION 5.2:** Create clarity of purpose, process, and product.
- **ACTION 5.3:** Create clarity through protocols.

## ACTION 5.1: CREATE CLARITY FOR SHARED UNDERSTANDING

What is clarity, and why is it important to PLCs? Put simply, *clarity* is clearness. Being clear gives direction, meaning, focus, and synergy to what school leaders are trying to achieve. Without it, we often face roadblocks, obstacles, and ambiguity. When dealing with change, clarity helps us put one foot in front of the other until we achieve what we are striving for. Anyone can have an idea, but without clarity on the strategic execution of that idea, a school will make very little progress.

In PLCs, clarity is particularly important, as leaders, educators, and students create, share, build, and manage collaborative learning environments for themselves and others. For students, clarity about what learning goals they are striving to achieve and how they can achieve these goals is an identified factor in student success (Hattie, 2009; Reeves, 2004; Wiliam, 2011). For educators, using assessments to gain clarity about where students are in their learning at a given time has a proven influence on achievement (Wiliam, 2011). And for leaders, the desire to translate a school mission and vision into reality means having the skill and clarity to bring vision to life (Wayman, Midgley, & Stringfield, 2006).

Indeed, Richard DuFour, Rebecca DuFour, and Robert Eaker (2008) remind us that a school cannot function as a PLC until staff members can clearly answer key questions about why their school exists—their mission—and how they will go about fulfilling their purpose, or vision. According to DuFour and his coauthors (2016), collaborative teams "engage in a systematic process in which they work together, interdependently, to analyze and impact their professional practice in order to improve individual and collective results" (p. 60). Clarity is of paramount importance. Without clarity, school improvement strategies often become unsustainable, ineffective, and unmanageable.

For an example of the impact that clarity can have on a school's progress toward becoming a PLC, consider the following instance of a school leadership team who makes the common mistake of failing to establish a clear purpose and process for its chosen school improvement strategy.

The school leadership team at a rural primary school is discussing the notion of collaboration. Team members have noticed that a prominent theme in recent policy documents and research has been the effectiveness of collaborative learning in the development of teachers' knowledge, skills, and understandings. Through some reflective discussions, they realize that their current culture is not collaborative; instead, teachers at the school typically work in isolation to plan and assess student learning.

The leadership team feels that teachers will work more effectively if they meet regularly in collaborative teams. They decide that instead of the weekly communication meetings held each Tuesday afternoon, teachers will meet with their colleagues who teach the same grade level and focus their attention on student learning. These meetings will also help with the school improvement goals set out in the leadership team's annual implementation plan.

At the next staff meeting, the principal shares this new structure with teachers, explaining that the new meetings will begin the following week. Teachers are less than enthused about their new meeting structure, but they begin the meeting process as instructed. Two weeks later, the leadership team meets back to reflect on the new meeting structure and reports that teachers are unmotivated and unclear on what the meetings are expected to achieve. There is an overall consensus among educators that the PLC process is just another fad that will soon pass.

The previous example highlights a common problem in schools. The leadership team tries to rush the improvement strategy and does not pay attention to building shared understanding of the purpose of collaborative teams, the processes they should undertake, or the products they are to develop. They do not use data to inform a focus for the teams, and reasons for the change are not clear to staff.

Consider a school leadership team that had, instead, worked over a period of time with staff to engage in professional readings and dialogue. Leaders had analyzed data to determine a focus area for the collaboration, and then established clear and carefully considered processes for teams to utilize during meetings. In this scenario, the kind of effective collaboration that leads to improved student learning would be more likely to develop.

## ACTION 5.2: CREATE CLARITY OF PURPOSE, PROCESS, AND PRODUCT

It is the school leader's role to create and establish the clarity of purpose, process, and products necessary to ensure lucidity in the staff members' understandings about the PLC process and implement clear school improvement strategies that are purposeful and sustainable.

## CLARITY OF PURPOSE

People engage in learning when there is a purpose to do so. Understanding the fundamental reason for why we do what we do is therefore imperative to success. When students have a clear rationale for their learning, they are more likely to achieve success (Clarke, Timperley, & Hattie, 2003), and the same can be said for educators. The following scenario shows what happens when purpose is not clear.

In the staffroom of a large suburban secondary school, the principal, Ngaire, commences the first staff meeting for the year. On the agenda is the development of team norms to support collaboration in the school's collaborative teams. Ngaire begins by explaining that she would like each team to spend dedicated time in its first team meeting developing a small set of norms that will be lived and transparent in their meetings. She shows her staff some effective and practical processes that they can use to develop their norms and concludes by sharing some examples of team norms.

The following week, teams of teachers get together to develop their team norms. They collectively choose one of the processes that Ngaire showed the week before and use the examples as scaffolds for the development of their norms. They feel clear about the process and products that they are being asked to develop.

Later in the term, Ngaire begins to notice that some of the teams are facing difficulties. During weekly catch-ups with the team facilitators, she observes many discussions based on the difficulties that leaders are experiencing when reinforcing team norms. This has often resulted in ineffective team meetings, with colleagues frequently arriving late, unprepared, or unwilling to contribute. Although most team norms are focused on areas of attendance, collective efficacy, and collaboration, it is apparent that some team members are not living the norms they have set.

When reflecting on this difficulty, Ngaire begins to question her method of introducing team norms to her staff. Although she had provided her colleagues with clear examples and processes for the development of norms, she had not clarified why teams were being asked to develop them or why they were essential in creating a collaborative culture. She had focused on the process and product of norms but had not led her colleagues to identify a purpose or rationale for their implementation. As a consequence, the norms have no impact on the professional behaviors because some team members don't see them as relevant.

The situation in this school reflects one of the pervasive challenges in PLCs. While most educators do their best to provide relevant and meaningful instruction to their students, and most leaders do their best to deliver purposeful communications to their staff, lack of clarity often means they maintain the status quo.

Reculturing a school as a PLC requires time and energy as the community navigates unfamiliar territory in teaching and learning practices. If educators don't see a clear purpose, they are more likely to give up and revert to old practices that reflect the way in which things have always been done. However, when educators are clear and see value in what the school is trying to achieve—high levels of learning for all students—the effort and time required to transform into a PLC becomes more manageable and meaningful.

Leaders must be vigilant in ensuring that when they ask their staff to engage in change, they provide them with a clear purpose for undertaking the change in the first place. This includes collectively discussing how the change aligns with the school's mission and vision statements as outlined in chapter 4 (page 55).

## CLARITY OF PROCESS

While clarity of purpose provides a rationale for change, ultimately a school cannot enact its vision if school leaders are not clear on the process it will use to achieve it. Leaders in a PLC therefore make collective commitments to the processes they will undertake to achieve their goals. These processes enable educators to contribute to the common goal of creating a culture and structures focused on improving student learning. When educators are clear on processes that are aligned to their purpose, they then are more likely to carry them out with the fidelity required. For example, think about the following scenario.

A team of grade 2 teachers identifies that in order to work toward the school's fundamental purpose of ensuring all students learn at high levels, it needs to redirect its focus. The teachers decide to collectively commit to designing and implementing a plan to ensure that all students who are struggling in an upcoming literacy unit of work will receive the additional time and instruction required to reach mastery. However, to ensure this commitment is successful, the team needs to be clear on the processes it will undertake. The team therefore agrees to administer and analyze multiple common assessment tasks throughout the unit of work to determine student learning needs. This includes identifying tasks for the assessment and dates when it will take place.

continued →

> The team of teachers then goes about creating a process through which it can respond to the results in a timely and meaningful manner. It designs a timetable that allows each teacher to work flexibly within his or her classroom by grouping together students with similar needs and providing relevant and effective instruction to support each group of students to reach mastery in the concepts being taught. This assessment and instructional cycle is complemented by additional interventions from learning support staff to provide additional time and support to students who are at risk of not reaching proficiency. All groups implement ongoing assessment to monitor the effectiveness of the teaching and learning. The team members constantly reflect on these results and respond to them in weekly team meetings.

The process that this team of teachers creates is one that uses assessment to determine the best instruction for all students and ensure that all students are learning at a level of proficiency. In order to be effective, all members of the team need to understand and agree on the process that is required to reach their goal. Without clarity of process, there are likely to be discrepancies among the actions that team members take to resolve the issue. This ultimately makes it impossible for the team to collectively respond to the assessment data in a systematic and collaborative manner. We are not suggesting that *all* processes teams develop must be in unison with one another—but when educators work collaboratively on the work that matters to student learning, it is imperative that they establish clear and manageable processes.

Clarity of process also provides a reference point for collaborative teams when they discuss their progress toward team goals. In PLCs, educators engage in ongoing reflection to monitor their success. DuFour and his colleagues (2008) suggest that as a result of this cycle:

> Educators in a PLC engage in collective inquiry into (1) best practices about teaching and learning; (2) a candid clarification of their current practices; and (3) an honest assessment of their students' current levels of learning. (p. 16)

When educators are clear on the series of actions they will take to reach a specific goal, then they can also identify whether steps in the process are ineffective and need to change. If they are clear on what it takes to reach their goals, then all members of the team will feel more competent and efficacious in their practice (Gregory & Kuzmich, 2007).

## CLARITY OF PRODUCT

The generation of products forms part of the work of a PLC. Educators and leaders develop products to support collaboration, learning, and results. For instance, to support collaboration, members of a PLC develop norms to help navigate the professional learning conversations that occur during collaborative team meetings. Similarly, common assessment tasks are designed so that educators can continually monitor the effectiveness of teaching and learning on the basis of learning data. What is fundamental to the success of these products is a consistency between the products that are developed from team to team.

While it is expected that teams will create different products from one another in response to the students they are working with, products developed should show some consistency from team to team. This consistency creates a systematic approach to best practice in which collaborative teams, although they remain responsive to their students' unique needs, are working toward a shared vision based on the PLC mission of high levels of learning for all students. In order to achieve this consistency in products, members of PLCs need to be clear on what products are effective in their work. Take the example in the following scenario.

A small secondary school is working toward developing data protocols to aid the analysis of data from common assessment tasks. Currently, each team undertakes data analysis very differently. Some teams analyze data as a team, while others do so as individuals. The school leadership team therefore asks the teams to develop data protocols that will help them analyze formative and summative data in an ongoing and collective manner.

However, as each team goes about creating these products, leaders notice that effectiveness varies from team to team. One team finds a data protocol in a book that helps teachers identify the strengths and weaknesses of student learning but does not encourage them to reflect on their own practice. Another team of teachers designs a protocol that extracts data from assessment tasks to reflect on teaching and learning but does not encourage teachers to use the data analysis to identify action in their classrooms.

The school's leadership team does not want to enforce a rule that all teams must use the same data protocol—mainly because different assessment tasks may require dissimilar analysis. However, they are committed to ensuring that the data protocols used by teams reflect best practice in data analysis and ultimately lead to improved teaching and learning results.

The leadership team decides that the data protocol may be different from team to team but must include some non-negotiables. After engaging in readings and discussion using research and examples of data protocols, it identifies a criterion that each team must include in its final product.

In the previous example, school leaders ensure that each staff member is clear on common characteristics of the product, but they also make room for some flexibility in the design of the product to reflect the variations in data from each key learning area. This approach ensures commonality in agreed-on practices, but it also makes it possible for educators to modify their final product to suit their context.

Product development takes time, commitment, and a relentless process of inquiry into best practice. Leaders of PLCs must ensure that time and effort is not wasted on the creation of ineffective products that do not lead to improvements in student learning. Instead, leaders must guide their colleagues to access relevant information to support product generation, so that each team creates effective products that are successful, useful, and aligned to the school's mission and vision.

## ALIGNMENT OF PURPOSE, PROCESS, AND PRODUCT

School leaders can have a clear mission and vision for their school, but without clarity among all stakeholders about the right strategies and agreed implementation, they will make very little progress. When leaders fall into the trap of being ambiguous about the purpose, process, and products of both cultural and structural changes, intentions become questionable, doubt begins to fester, and efforts decrease. Leaders should carefully and strategically consider the culture they are trying to achieve and the structures that are required to support them to achieve such a culture. When all members of a school are clear about the purpose of what they are working on, the processes they would use, and the products that are expected, then they are more likely to be successful in the change process. The success of this process relies on the clarity that leaders can provide.

# ACTION 5.3: CREATE CLARITY THROUGH PROTOCOLS

Clarity in purpose, process, and product is of great significance in reculturing schools to become PLCs. However, a major factor that can affect clarity is communication. One tool that school leaders can use to ensure clear communication, especially within collaborative teams, is protocols to enhance professional dialogue. Protocols allow school leaders to foster a culture that is rich in communication. This allows communication to go beyond sharing to professional challenge and inquiry. In action 5.3 we will first provide some background about the use of protocols in a PLC and then share four protocols that educators can use to grow the collaborative dialogue of a PLC.

## THE ROLE OF DIALOGUE IN TRANSFORMATIVE COLLABORATION

Research into dialogue highlights the importance of learning about oneself and others through discussing experiences, theories, hopes, and fears (Clark, 2001; Dalton, 2010). Leading social constructivists such as Albert Bandura (1993), Jerome Bruner (1985) and Jean Piaget (1973) place dialogue at the center of learning, as they understand learning to be a social process. More recently, Parry Graham (2007) describes how within a collaborative team structure, dialogue is the foundation of the learning community, since it is the medium through which all information is exchanged. These theories and beliefs are significant within a PLC, where collaborative dialogue is paramount to learning.

Dialogue, according to educational policy professor Nicholas C. Burbules (1993), must encapsulate at least two points of view and requires participants to mediate between more than one perspective. It is within this mediation that clarity of intention and meaning is vital—for without it, relationships between colleagues can be broken. Education professor Christopher M. Clark (2001) employs criteria for teacher conversations to ensure different viewpoints are heard. The criteria include:

- Articulating implicit theories and beliefs
- Developing a sense of personal and professional identity
- Receiving hope and relational connections
- Reaffirming ideals and commitments
- Developing specific techniques and solutions to problems
- Learning how to engage in learning conversations

These criteria are a useful frame that leaders can use to reflect on the current state of dialogue within collaborative teams and set goals for future development. Leaders should be clear on the strategies that they can use to encourage professional discussion that centers on teaching and learning. Protocols allow collaborative teams to hold each other accountable for instructional practice and results, respect each other's opinions and, most importantly, believe that they are always capable of improving their own practice (Elmore, 2004; Fullan, 2001).

## USING PROTOCOLS TO SUPPORT COLLABORATIVE DIALOGUE

Engaging in dialogue about student learning and teaching practice in ways that will lead to improved learning results is essential to school improvement. As Elizabeth A. City, Richard F. Elmore, Sarah E. Fiarman, and Lee Teitel (2009) explain, "The problem is not that the schools don't have access to knowledge. The problem is that they don't have a process of translating that knowledge systematically into practice" (p. 9). Professional conversations may become shallow because the language does not support a collaborative understanding of teaching and learning. This suggests that the language in collaborative interactions can become a barrier to developing common understandings.

One way to overcome this obstacle is through the use of protocols. According to principal and author Catherine Glaude (2011), "A protocol is a process for guiding a professional learning conversation. The purpose of a protocol is to build the skills and promote the culture necessary for ongoing collaborative learning" (p. 2). Glaude (2011) offers the following list of traits to explain how protocols can support clear and effective dialogue in professional learning conversations:

A protocol:

- Keeps a group conversation focused in order to generate a wealth of helpful conversation and feedback in a limited amount of time

- Encourages all members of the group to offer their most thoughtful and useful feedback and insights on a specific topic

- Helps less verbal participants offer their voices into the conversation

- Promotes thoughtfulness by allowing personal reflection time within a group conversation

- Encourages lively dialogue featuring multiple perspectives

- Requires any individuals presenting their personal work to remain silent so that the feedback and insights offered from their colleagues are not lost

- Reminds individuals to return to the evidence offered in the text or the video, rather than offering opinions, when conversations are focused on current research

- Provides a safe and supportive structure for all to inspect their practices and results of the learning (p. 2)

While protocols can vary in purpose and process, they ultimately provide a clear and transparent structure that promotes conversation among colleagues. David Allen and Tina Blythe (2004) suggest that while protocols may appear simple on the surface, they are in reality quite complex. They explain that protocols are designed to "help configure—not script—an experience through which individuals and the group as a whole can learn" (p. 10). Joseph P. McDonald, Nancy Mohr, Alan Dichter, and Elizabeth C. McDonald (2015) suggest that protocols "force transparency by segmenting elements of a conversation whose boundaries often blur" (p. 7). Protocols make positive feedback credible and constructive feedback tolerable. They help members of a PLC engage in deep and sometimes challenging dialogue, listen meaningfully to others' opinions, and take action if required.

## USING PROTOCOLS IN A COLLABORATIVE TEAM

Building a PLC requires teams of educators to engage in ongoing reflective conversations about student learning and teacher practice. In these conversations, educators must consider the instructional decisions they have made and examine factors that affect these decisions. By participating in such conversations, educators develop cognitive dispositions that they might not have been able to develop working in isolation.

The implementation of protocols ensures that focused conversations become the norm and "individuals become skillful in learning together" (Glaude, 2011, p. 2). Protocols encourage educators to take charge of their learning by using inside perspectives from their own and their colleagues' reflections to build shared understandings of practice. Some protocols also incorporate outside sources of information—such as professional readings—to aid colleagues to access, understand, and adjust practices according to expert opinions (McDonald et al., 2015). Ultimately, protocols leverage the knowledge and experience of educators to solve their own problems and build their professional practice in collaboration with their colleagues. Protocols provide a clear process to elicit tacit knowledge—the intuitive knowledge that is grounded in context and experience—and reflect on and sometimes challenge current thinking using a safe and meaningful structure.

## CHOOSING THE RIGHT PROTOCOL TO SUIT THE PURPOSE

There is an abundance of protocols available for educators to use in collaborative teams. Some protocols support collaborative teams to work through problems of practice, while others aid in the analysis of student work samples and data. Choosing an appropriate protocol to suit the purpose is essential to success.

When considering what protocol would suit the team's purpose, it is important to contemplate aspects such as number of participants, time available, resources required, and, most important, the expected outcome. Some protocols can be easily administered in a short amount of time with few resources or little preparation. Others require careful planning and preparation. Simply implementing a protocol in an ad hoc manner may not lead to improved dialogue and reflection among colleagues. Instead, educators should consider the purpose of their focus and the products they want to develop, and then identify a process that will enable them to meet their goals. For example, a team may want to focus on improving the ways it resolves issues as a team. The members want a relatively short protocol that they can use and trust whenever they come up against issues that require careful and strategic problem solving. They could use the Peeling the Onion Protocol (McDonald et al., 2015) discussed later in this chapter to assist their team in dealing with problems or conflicts that arise as a natural part of the change process.

## IMPLEMENTING PROTOCOLS WITH FIDELITY

One important aspect of protocols is to trust the process. When teams begin to use protocols, they can sometimes feel artificial and clumsy because they disrupt the natural flow of conversation. However, this disturbance is intentional. Protocols are designed to turn natural conversations into structured, highly reflective dialogues that create time for talking and listening, provide boundaries to restrict judgment and disrespectful behaviors, and afford opportunities for both individual and group learning to occur (Allen & Blythe, 2004). Regular practice is therefore essential.

When initially implementing protocols, there is a tendency for collaborative teams to divert from the original guidelines or steps and replace them with more natural dialogue. While this natural dialogue may be effective, all too often it can lead to unproductive results.

Interruptions, distractions, dominance by some team members, or lack of participation by others may ultimately affect the outcomes—as too may the lack of evidence to support thinking. It is therefore important to implement protocols with fidelity and accuracy to the guidelines. One way to support this implementation is to appoint a facilitator for the process.

## ROLE OF FACILITATOR WHEN IMPLEMENTING THE PROTOCOL

A facilitator's role is to maintain commitment and support colleagues to believe in the protocol's capacity to create a space where group members can learn together (Allen & Blythe, 2004). At the heart of the role of the facilitator, then, is the ability and skill to support participation and success through equity and trusting relationships (McDonald et al., 2015). Facilitators should be firm but supportive in protocol implementation by encouraging full participation and ensuring that all members of the team feel respected and safe as they participate. This means helping colleagues understand the purpose, process, and products of the protocol and creating an environment where all members are responsible and accountable for the team's actions.

At times, the facilitator may be required to encourage a member to participate more or suggest that another member listens more attentively to others. A facilitator may be required to guide conversations by providing prompts, connecting ideas, or paraphrasing responses to ensure that everyone achieves clarity. Often, a facilitator will need to open and conclude the protocol.

McDonald and colleagues (2015) suggest facilitators should aim to support team members to contribute early and in ways that will connect all members to the focus of the conversation. This prevents uncomfortable silences and dominant behaviors. They also suggest that facilitators close protocols by considering three questions:

- **WHAT?** What have I learnt about the topic that brought this team together?

- **SO WHAT?** What difference does it seem to make—for example, to my teaching or my team's planning?

- **NOW WHAT?** What steps can I take to make the most of what I have learned? (McDonald et al., 2015, p. 20)

While the role of the facilitator is significant to the success of the protocol, it is important for all members of the team to understand that the protocol is not a solution but instead a practice that, over time, the team can harness and embed in regular conversations.

## PROTOCOLS THAT SCHOOLS ARE USING IN PLCS

Schools we have worked with that are transforming into PLCs are successfully implementing a range of protocols to support learning dialogue. In this section, we briefly explore how four of the more common protocols can be adopted by teams to support clear and effective conversations about student learning. These protocols are as follows.

- Tuning Protocol
- Peeling the Onion Protocol
- Three Levels of Text Protocol
- Looking at Data Protocol

## Tuning Protocol

The Tuning Protocol (McDonald et al., 2015) is a facilitated process that aids educators to share and discuss student work. Typically, a member of the team shares student work with the team members without interruption from colleagues. Team members then have time to examine the work, ask clarifying questions, and provide feedback that is both supportive (warm) and challenging (cool). The presenter has the opportunity to address the feedback and debrief about the process. The role of the facilitator is to encourage all team members to be respectful listeners and contributors to the dialogue.

Frequently, schools use the Tuning Protocol to help determine whether students have learned what they have been taught. Using students' work samples, teams of teachers reflect on and analyze the student responses to determine whether teaching and learning has been successful. In employing the Tuning Protocol, teams use highly reflective conversations and evidence of student learning to monitor and check the effectiveness of teacher practice.

The Tuning Protocol takes forty-five minutes to an hour or more. The guidelines that follow are for an hour-long session, which is common. Usually six to twelve participants are involved, though the protocol is sometimes used by groups as large as thirty. Presenters might share relevant supporting materials, which may include documents in paper or video format. The steps of the Tuning Protocol, adapted from McDonald and colleagues (2015), are as follows.

- **INTRODUCTION:** The facilitator briefly introduces the protocol goals and norms and distributes a copy of the steps. (Five minutes)

- **PRESENTATION:** The presenter shares the problem, or a draft of a plan currently under development, and provides relevant information about efforts to date. The presenter may also highlight particular questions that he or she would like the respondents to address, drawing on documents as appropriate to support the presentation. During this step, respondents may not speak. (Fifteen minutes)

- **RESPONSE:** Respondents note their warm and cool reactions to what the presenter has said. Warm reactions emphasize the strength of the presenter's views of the problem and his or her particular approaches to solving it. Cool reactions emphasize problematic aspects of these. Often cool reactions come in the form of questions: "I'm wondering why you chose to . . . " or "I'm curious about your interpretation of the parental reaction. Could you say more?" During this step, the presenter may not speak. He or she is encouraged instead to take notes, and in the process to consider which responses to comment on and which to let pass. In some versions of the Tuning Protocol, participants are invited to offer warm reactions first, then cool. In other versions, participants are encouraged to mix warm and cool (though never in the same response). (Fifteen minutes)

■ **REACTION:** The presenter reacts to any responses he or she chooses to react to. The facilitator reminds the presenter that the response is not meant to answer questions but to talk about her or his thinking. During this step, respondents may not speak. (Ten minutes)

■ **CONVERSATION:** Presenter and respondents engage in open conversation. (Ten minutes)

■ **DEBRIEFING:** Participants reflect on the process and explore ways to use the protocol in other situations. The facilitator may ask, "How did it feel hearing warm and cool feedback? How did it feel not being able to respond to the feedback? How can you apply this protocol in your ordinary work?" (Five minutes)

### Peeling the Onion Protocol

Solving problems is an ongoing issue for any collaborative team. The various opinions, perspectives, and experiences of a diverse range of team members are what make for successful collaboration, but they can also be the cause of unresolved conflict. Using problem-solving protocols such as Peeling the Onion (McDonald et al., 2015) encourages teams to frame problems for collaborative review.

Peeling the Onion is a structured method that supports educators as they solve problems collaboratively. The protocol helps colleagues peel away the layers of a problem so that they can get to the crux of the issue. The role of the facilitator is important in this protocol, as people have a natural tendency to offer solutions instead of gradually unpacking the problem. The facilitator must ensure that participants listen, reflect, and pose questions instead of suggesting resolutions.

In collaborative teams, educators have used this protocol and others similar to it when dealing with a range of challenges. At times, the challenge at hand may be a personal issue that is based on the relationships within the team, but more often the focus is on working through problems of practice in teaching and learning. Educators commonly use such protocols to identify teaching strategies that they can implement to support students who are having difficulties with learning.

The protocol takes approximately forty minutes and is best for a group of ten to twelve members. The steps, adapted from McDonald and colleagues (2015), are as follows.

- **SHARING THE PROBLEM:** Someone agrees to share a problem that he or she needs help with. (five minutes)

- **CLARIFYING QUESTIONS:** Only clarifying questions may be asked—ones that elicit brief additional explanation. (three minutes)

- **ACTIVE LISTENING:** The facilitator goes around the room and has everyone complete the statement: "I understand the problem to be . . . " The presenter stays silent and takes notes. (ten minutes)

- **PEELING AND PROBING:** The facilitator goes around the room again and has everyone pose additional questions raised from the first round. (ten minutes)

- **RESPONSE:** The facilitator invites a response from the presenter as follows: "Having heard these questions, please share any new thoughts about the problem you presented." (five minutes)

- **OPEN CONVERSATION:** The facilitator invites the group to have an open conversation. (five minutes)

- **DEBRIEFING:** The facilitator prompts: "How was this like peeling an onion? What other 'onions' do you imagine peeling?" (two minutes)

## Three Levels of Text Protocol

Professional reading is an important part of educator learning. By engaging in professional reading, educators can connect with new ideas, identify the latest research, and reflect on their practices in comparison with those of others. Engaging in professional reading with colleagues is a supportive and worthwhile activity as it gives teachers the space and time to deeply engage with the main ideas in the professional reading. The Three Levels of Text Protocol (Easton, 2009) supports teams of teachers to collaboratively construct meaning and to clarify and extend their thinking about a reading.

The Three Levels of Text Protocol encourages participants to read short sections of a text and highlight key words, phrases, and sentences. Then, with the support of a facilitator, participants share these connections by explaining their importance. A whole-team discussion follows in which team members discuss what these main ideas mean for their practice. The protocol concludes with a debrief.

Collaborative teams use protocols like the Three Levels of Text Protocol when researching and inquiring into best practice. Educators are constantly barraged with ideas, strategies, and activities, but many of these ideas are not created according to an evidence-based instructional model. Educators in collaborative teams constantly question, critique, and inquire into best practice to ensure that the opportunities they provide their students are the best possible practices that will lead to high levels of learning. A protocol such as Three Levels of Text supports educators to identify effective assessment practices and understand complex instructional approaches. In reading and discussing such issues in a collaborative team environment, the team builds shared understandings and critiques resources and strategies before implementation occurs.

The ideal group size is six to ten participants, so if the whole group is larger, it should be broken into subgroups. There is no presenter in this protocol, but there should be a facilitator. It is also helpful to have a recorder who will chart what people say.

Teams can complete this protocol in as few as twenty minutes, and they can extend it for as long as there is time. In fact, the protocol should be extended if the text the team is examining is long and complex or if there are more than ten people in a group. The suggested times in the protocol steps that follow are based on a forty-five-minute session. The steps of the protocol, adapted from Easton (2009), are as follows.

- **INTRODUCING THE TEXT:** This step may occur before the participants meet or at the beginning of the session. Participants read, view, or listen to the text and take notes. (Time depends on length and complexity of text)

- **SENTENCES:** Each member of the group selects a sentence that he or she finds significant from the text (if the text is written) or from notes (if the text is aural or visual). The other participants listen and take notes on what each person says, but there is no discussion. (Ten minutes)

- **PHRASES:** Each member of the group selects a phrase that he or she finds significant from the text (if the text is written) or from notes (if the text is aural or visual). The other participants listen and take notes on what each person says, but there is no discussion. (Ten minutes)

- **WORDS:** Each member of the group selects a word that he or she finds significant from the text (if the text is written) or from notes (if the text is aural or visual). The other participants listen and take notes on what each person says, but there is no discussion. (Ten minutes)

- **DISCUSSION:** Participants discuss what they heard and what they've learned about the text they studied. (Ten minutes)

- **DEBRIEFING:** The group debriefs the process. (Five minutes)

## Looking at Data Protocol

Collaborative teams use data to improve learning. Teams of teachers use these data to respond to and monitor the success of teaching, learning, and leadership. However, analyzing data isn't always an easy process. It requires patience, organization, and, most importantly, the time and resources to respond to the findings.

The Looking at Data Protocol (McDonald et al., 2015) guides teams of educators to analyze student data and identify the strengths and challenges of practice. The protocol begins by inviting participants to identify the facts associated with the data without engaging in collaborative conversation. After the facts have been identified, the facilitator supports the team to dig deeper by offering additional thoughts about the data and providing evidence. Following this, participants identify strengths and problems using the data and conclude by offering recommendations for addressing the data.

Collaborative teams use the Looking at Data Protocol for a range of purposes. The protocol is useful when schools are working on their mission and vision. Using large data sets such as standardized assessment data and parent and student opinion surveys, educators can identify priorities for the school and set directions for further attention. The protocol also helps schools monitor progress toward goals that they have previously set and engage in reflection, redirection, and celebration through analysis.

The protocol can be completed in one hour or less, depending on the number of participants (four to ten or more), and the times allotted to each step. In the version we present, one participant serves as presenter, another as facilitator, and a third as recorder. The steps of the protocol, adapted from McDonald and colleagues (2015), are as follows.

- **PLANNING:** The presenter familiarizes him- or herself with the data set in preparation for orientation. This may in some circumstances require expert support. (Time as needed)

- **ORIENTATION:** The presenter offers an orientation to the data set. This may include, for example, what the columns, rows, and cells contain, what abbreviations mean, how best to read the tables, and so on. The facilitator asks participants to hold questions for the next step. (Three minutes)

- **FOCUS QUESTION:** The presenter suggests a focus question for the group's reading of the data. This is likely one that is related to a priority that the group or school has set. (Three minutes)

- **CLARIFYING QUESTIONS:** Participants ask questions on matters that they find unclear or confusing. If the presenter cannot easily answer, and if collective pondering yields little, then the questions are deferred for later expert consultation. (Five minutes)

- **FLAGGING:** Participants work in teams of two or three to call attention to particular data within the data set that may prove especially relevant to the focus question. They do not necessarily need to explain why they think attention is warranted. The recorder notes the flagged data—for example, by highlighting cells. Discussion is not permitted at this point. (Ten minutes)

- **MAKING INFERENCES:** Participants work in teams of two or three to make inferences based on particular elements of the data set. Again, no discussion is permitted. The recorder records all the inferences on poster paper or by computer projection. (Ten minutes)

- **DISCUSSION:** The facilitator invites open discussion about both the data elements that surfaced in the clarifying questioning and the inferences that surfaced during flagging. The recorder continues to record. (Ten minutes or more)
- **STEPPING BACK:** Going around the room, participants state briefly what they see as next steps for the group, given their analysis and discussion. These may include additional clarification, further inquiry, or action. (Five to ten minutes)

# REFLECTION

Every PLC leader wants to see the school's vision become a reality. Clarity in leader communications, perceptions, thoughts, and actions remain the key to achieving this. Only through clarity will the school community be able to organize its thinking and actions to achieve positive results. Coupled with the ability to translate a clear vision into straightforward values and goals, clarity also produces a leadership style where colleagues and the community trust and connect to the leadership of the school.

At the team level, teachers must be clear regarding the common issues surrounding curriculum, assessment, instruction, and the achievement of all students (Marzano et al., 2014). In action 5.3, we shared examples of protocols that can support teams of teachers to develop this clarity.

# REFLECTIVE QUESTIONS: COMMITMENT 5— CREATE CLARITY ABOUT COLLABORATION

As you consider each reflective question, contemplate your response and identify the evidence that supports your thinking.

## ACTION 5.1: CREATE CLARITY FOR SHARED UNDERSTANDING

- What opportunities are there for teachers and leaders to discuss and clarify their understanding of becoming a PLC?
- To what extent do staff at your school understand the purpose of collaborative teams?

## ACTION 5.2: CREATE CLARITY OF PURPOSE, PROCESS, AND PRODUCT

- To what extent do staff demonstrate a clear understanding of the mission and vision of the school?
- What measures have school leaders taken to provide clear and transparent communication to staff in support of collaborative teamwork?
- Are changes in behaviors, practices, or resources at your school effectively managed by creating clarity on the purpose, process, and products of change?

## ACTION 5.3: CREATE CLARITY THROUGH PROTOCOLS

- How have school leaders provided the necessary support, conditions, and protocols to foster collaborative dialogue that challenges existing practice?
- In what ways has this led to agreed-on and common understandings among teams?
- What protocols does your school use to support collaboration or curriculum, assessment, and instruction?

# INSIGHTS FROM THE FIELD

*We regularly use protocols to help support the teams in what they're doing. Two leadership meetings ago, we used a team-analysis protocol where the team members rate themselves out of ten, and then we ask them all to come up with two or three things that were stretching them or that they were having difficulty with.*

*The PLC journey has changed my leadership because I've got a much clearer focus on where we're going as a school. Putting things in place previously was more ad hoc. It was like a band-aid approach to things, whereas I think the PLC gives us clear direction, and I think it's easier to articulate that direction since everyone understands where we're going and what we're trying to do. For me, I think it's given me clearer direction as a leader. I know where we want to go. It's given us a focus for the school: a clear focus and a positive focus.*

—DREW, PRINCIPAL

*I think in a team environment it is a case of always talking the talk so that everybody is on the same page. It is about making it clear from the word go that the PLC process is all about the learning. The bigger picture is learning, but it's also important to keep that talk happening within every conversation.*

—IVY, ASSISTANT PRINCIPAL

*It's the talking. It's the celebration of the small steps toward transformation through the data we gather on student learning, through the feedback we're getting from staff. It's stopping and asking ourselves, "OK, are we moving forward?" We've got a long way to go, and we always say that, but it's about being clear about those small incremental steps that we're making toward our goal.*

*And it's being explicit in that talk to remind the staff of where they were. People get swept up in the journey, and they only remember where they are at the present time and forget where they actually came from. It's going back and saying, "Remember when we raised this last time? We had no idea, and now you've got this much clearer idea of it." It's reminding the educators of how much they have grown. When you're immersed in it, you don't see the growth, so our role as leaders is to make sure the staff understand. When we talk about intervention, they go, "Oh, it's not quite right, we haven't got it right." We respond with, "Well, look where you were a year ago."*

—CHRIS, PRINCIPAL

# GLOSSARY OF COLLABORATION TERMS AND DEFINITIONS

**clarity.** The clearness of purpose, process, and product that gives direction, meaning, focus, and synergy to what PLC members are trying to achieve.

**collaboration.** When colleagues in a school come together to share ideas, tools, and strategies in order to make key curriculum, assessment, instruction, teaching, and leadership decisions.

**collaborative team.** When educators within a PLC form smaller collaborative groups that meet on a regular basis to share knowledge, analyze data, and generate new ways of functioning in order to best support the students they serve.

**collegiality.** A style of team engagement that prioritizes strong professional relationships among fellow educators.

**coordination.** A style of team engagement that involves organizing diverse elements together in a congruous operation.

**culture.** "The deeper level of basic assumptions and beliefs that are shared by members of an organization, that operate unconsciously, and that define in a basic 'take-for-granted' fashion an organization's view of itself and its environment" (Schein, 1985, p. 6).

**distributed leadership.** A method of leadership that concentrates on collaborative interaction between individuals in formal and informal leadership roles, sharing out some leadership and management responsibilities while keeping the leadership team at the center of operations.

**first-order change.** Change that is gradual and incremental as opposed to dramatic and sweeping (see *second-order change*).

**instructional leadership.** A style of leadership in which the leader focuses on the direct impact of teachers on student outcomes.

**norm.** A collective commitment that prescribes how team members will behave during collaborative team meetings.

**PLC.** See *professional learning community*.

**professional development.** A form of vocational training in which teachers are positioned as the passive recipients of predetermined knowledge or skills.

**professional learning.** A form of vocational training that requires teachers to take an active role in the co-construction of professional knowledge.

**professional learning community.** "A group of connected and engaged professionals who are responsible for driving change and improvement within, between and across schools that will directly benefit learners" (Harris & Jones, 2010, p. 173).

**protocol.** "A process for guiding a professional learning conversation . . . to build the skills and promote the culture necessary for ongoing collaborative learning" (Glaude, 2011, p. 2).

**second-order change.** Change that is dramatic and sweeping as opposed to gradual and incremental (see *first-order change*).

**SMART goal.** Acronym for a goal that promotes a focus on results (S—Strategic and specific, M—Measurable, A—Attainable, R—Results oriented, T—Time bound; Conzemius & O'Neill, 2014).

**structures.** The organizational elements that make up a school.

**transformational leadership.** A style of leadership "in which the leaders take actions to increase their associates' awareness of what is right and important, to raise their associates' motivational maturity and to move their associates to go beyond the associates' own self-interests for the good of the group, organization, or society" (Bass & Avolio, 1996, p. 11).

**transformative collaboration.** The way in which PLCs utilize collaborative practice as the key lever for cultural and structural change that directly impacts student and teacher learning.

**trust.** "The social exchanges of schooling as organized around a distinct set of role relationships" (Bryk & Schneider, 2002, p. 20).

# REFERENCES AND RESOURCES

Allen, D., & Blythe, T. (2004). *The facilitator's book of questions: Tools for looking together at student and teacher work*. New York: Teachers College Press.

Bamburg, J. D., & Andrews, R. L. (1991). School goals, principals and achievement. *School Effectiveness and School Improvement, 2*(3), 175–191.

Bandura, A. (1993). Perceived self-efficacy in cognitive development and functioning. *Educational Psychologist, 28*(2), 117–148.

Bass, B., & Avolio, B. (1995). *Multifactor leadership questionnaire report*. Menlo Park, CA: Mind Garden.

Blase, J., & Kirby, P. C. (2000). *Bringing out the best in teachers: What effective principals do* (2nd ed.). Thousand Oaks, CA: Corwin Press.

Bruner, J. (1985). Vygotsky: An historical and conceptual perspective. In J. V. Wertsch (Ed.), *Culture, communication, and cognition: Vygotskian perspectives*, pp. 21–34. New York: Cambridge University Press.

Bryk, A. S., & Schneider, B. L. (2002). *Trust in schools: A core resource for improvement*. New York: Russell Sage Foundation.

Buffum, A., Mattos, M., & Malone, J. (2018). *Taking action: A handbook for RTI at Work*. Bloomington, IN: Solution Tree Press.

Burbules, N. C. (1993). *Dialogue in teaching: Theory and practice*. New York: Teachers College Press.

Carroll, L. (1865). *Alice's adventures in Wonderland*. Accessed at www.gutenberg.org/files/928/928-h/928-h.htm on July 31, 2020.

City, E. A., Elmore, R. F., Fiarman, S., & Teitel, L. (2009). *Instructional rounds in education: A network approach to improving teaching and learning*. Cambridge, MA: Harvard Education Press.

Clark, C. (Ed.). (2001). *Talking shop: Authentic conversations and teacher learning*. New York: Teachers College Press.

Clarke, S., Timperley, H., & Hattie, J. (2003). *Unlocking formative assessment: Practical strategies for enhancing students' learning in the primary and intermediate classroom*. London: Hodder & Stoughton.

Coggshall, J. G., Rasmussen, C., Colton, A., Milton, J., & Jacques, C. (2012). *Generating teaching effectiveness: The role of job-embedded professional learning in teacher evaluation*. Washington, DC: National Comprehensive Center for Teacher Quality. Accessed at http://files.eric.ed.gov/fulltext/ED532776.pdf on July 17, 2020.

Conzemius, A. E., & O'Neill, J. (2014). *The handbook for SMART school teams: Revitalizing best practices for collaboration*. Bloomington, IN: Solution Tree Press.

Covey, S. R. (2004). *The seven habits of highly effective people: Powerful lessons in personal change* (Rev. ed.). New York: Free Press.

Dalton, J. (2010). *Learning talk: Build understandings*. Maldon, VIC, Australia: Hands on Educational Consultancy.

De Dreu, C., & Van de Vliert, E. (Eds.). (1997). *Using conflict in organizations*. London: SAGE.

de Lima, J. Á. (2001). Forgetting about friendship: Using conflict in teacher communities as a catalyst for school change. *Journal of Educational Change, 2*, 97–122.

De Pree, M. (1989). *Leadership is an art*. New York: Doubleday.

Dinham, S. (2008). *Innovative and effective professional learning for student accomplishment* [PowerPoint presentation]. Accessed at www.slideserve.com/meryl/innovative-and-effective-professional-learning-for-student-accomplishment on July 28, 2020.

DuFour, R. (2004). What is a professional learning community? *Educational Leadership, 61*(8), 6–11. Accessed at www.ascd.org/publications/educational-leadership/may04/vol61/num08/What-Is-a-Professional-Learning-Community¢.aspx on July 17, 2020.

DuFour, R., DuFour, R., & Eaker, R. (2008). *Revisiting Professional Learning Communities at Work: New insights for improving schools*. Bloomington, IN: Solution Tree Press.

DuFour, R., DuFour, R., Eaker, R., & Many, T. W. (2006). *Learning by doing: A handbook for Professional Learning Communities at Work*. Bloomington, IN: Solution Tree Press.

DuFour, R., DuFour, R., Eaker, R., Many, T. W., & Mattos, M. (2016). *Learning by doing: A handbook for Professional Learning Communities at Work* (3rd ed.). Bloomington, IN: Solution Tree Press.

DuFour, R., & Fullan, M. (2013). *Cultures built to last: Systemic PLCs at Work*. Bloomington, IN: Solution Tree Press.

DuFour, R., & Marzano, R. J. (2011). *Leaders of learning: How district, school, and classroom leaders improve student achievement*. Bloomington, IN: Solution Tree Press.

DuFour, R., & Mattos, M. (2013). How do principals really improve schools? *Educational Leadership, 70*(7). Accessed at www.ascd.org/publications/educational-leadership/apr13/vol70/num07/How-Do-Principals-Really-Improve-Schools% C2% A2.aspx on July 17, 2020.

Dweck, C. S. (2008). *Mindset: The new psychology of success* (Rev. ed.). New York: Ballantine.

Easton, L. B. (2009). *Protocols for professional learning*. Alexandria, VA: Association for Supervision and Curriculum Development.

Edmonds, R. (1979). Effective schools for the urban poor. *Educational Leadership, 37*(1), 15–24.

Elmore, R. F. (2000). *Building a new structure for school leadership*. New York: Albert Shanker Institute.

Elmore, R. F. (2004). *School reform from the inside out: Policy, practice, and performance*. Cambridge, MA: Harvard University Press.

Evans, R. (1996). *The human side of school change: Reform, resistance, and the real-life problems of innovation*. San Francisco, CA: Jossey-Bass.

Fritz, R. (1984). *The path of least resistance: Learning to become the creative force in your own life*. Salem, MA: DMA.

Fullan, M. (1993). *Change forces: Probing the depths of educational reform*. New York: Falmer Press.

Fullan, M. (2001). *Leading in a culture of change*. San Francisco: Jossey-Bass.

Fullan, M. (2007). Change the terms for teacher learning. *Journal of Staff Development, 28*(3). Accessed at www.michaelfullan.ca/media/13396074650.pdf on July 17, 2020.

Fullan, M. (2008). *The six secrets of change: What the best leaders do to help their organizations survive and thrive*. San Francisco: Jossey-Bass.

Fullan, M. (2011). *Choosing the wrong drivers for whole school reform*. Seminar Series Paper No. 204, Centre for Strategic Education. Accessed at http://www.michaelfullan.ca/media/13396088160.pdf on 7/17/2020.

Galbraith, J. K. (1971). *Economics, peace and laughter: A contemporary guide*. Harmondsworth, UK: Penguin.

Glaude, C. (2011). *Protocols for professional learning conversations: Cultivating the art and discipline*. Bloomington, IN: Solution Tree Press.

Graham, P. (2007). The role of conversation, contention and commitment in a PLC. Accessed at http://cnx.org/content/m14270/1.1/ on 7/17/2020.

Gregory, G., & Kuzmich, L. (2007). *Teacher teams that get results*. Thousand Oaks, CA: Corwin Press.

Gurr, D. (2002). Transformational leadership characteristics in primary and secondary school principals. *Leading and Managing, 8*(1), 82–103.

Harris, A. (2014). *Distributed leadership matters: Perspectives, practicalities, and potential*, (Rev. ed.). Thousand Oaks, CA: Corwin Press.

Harris, A., & Jones, M. (2010). Professional learning communities and system improvement. *Improving Schools, 13*(2), 172–181.

Harris, A., & Jones, M. (2012). *Connecting professional learning: Leading effective collaborative enquiry across teaching school alliances.* Accessed at www.learnersfirst.net/private/wp-content/uploads/Connecting-professional-learning-leading-effective-collaborative-enquiry-across-teaching-school-alliances.pdf on July 28, 2020.

Harris, A., & Spillane, J. (2008). Distributed leadership through the looking glass. *Management in Education, 22*(1), 31–34. Accessed at www.sesp.northwestern.edu/docs/Harris_and_Spillane_-_Distributed_leadership_through_the_looking_glass.pdf on July 17, 2020.

Hattie, J. (2009). *Visible learning: A synthesis of over 800 meta-analyses relating to achievement.* New York: Routledge.

Hattie, J. (2012). *Visible learning for teachers: Maximizing impact on learning.* New York: Routledge.

Hierck, T., & Weber, C. (2014). *RTI is a verb.* Thousand Oaks, CA: Corwin Press.

Hipp, J., & Huffman, K. (2003). Professional learning communities: Assessment—development—effects. Paper presented at the International Congress for School Effectiveness and Improvement, Sydney, Australia.

Kanold, T. D. (2011). *The five disciplines of PLC leaders.* Bloomington, IN: Solution Tree Press.

Lashway, L. (2001). Leadership for accountability. *Research Roundup, 17*(3), 1–14.

Lave, J., & Wenger, E. (1991). *Situated learning: Legitimate peripheral participation.* New York: Cambridge University Press.

Learning Forward. (2015). *Standards for professional learning: learning communities.* Accessed at http://learningforward.org/standards/learning-communities#.VjA1c7yqpBc on July 17, 2020.

Lee, V. E., Smith, J. B., & Croninger, R. G. (1995). *Another look at high school restructuring: More evidence that it improves student achievement, and more insight into why.* (Issue Report No. 9). Madison: Center on Organization and Restructuring of Schools, University of Wisconsin.

Leithwood, K., Day, C., Sammons, P., Harris, A., & Hopkins, D. (2006). *Successful school leadership: What it is and how it influences pupil learning* (Research Report No. 800). Accessed at www.nysed.gov/common/nysed/files/principal-project-file-55-successful-school-leadership-what-it-is-and-how-it-influences-pupil-learning.pdf on July 30, 2020.

Leithwood, K., & Louis, K. S. (Eds.). (1999). *Organizational learning in schools.* Exton, PA: Swets and Zeitlinger.

Lezotte, L. W. (1991). *Correlates of effective schools: The first and second generation.* Okemos, MI: Effective Schools Products.

McDonald, J., Mohr, N., Dichter, A., & McDonald, E. (2015). *The power of protocols: An educator's guide to better practice.* New York: Teachers College Press.

Maraboli, S. (2014). *Life, the truth, and being free* (Rev. ed.). Port Washington, NY: A Better Today Publishing.

Marzano, R. J. (2003). *What works in schools: Translating research into action.* Alexandria, VA: Association for Supervision and Curriculum Development.

Marzano, R. J., Heflebower, T., Hoegh, J. K., Warrick, P., & Grift, G. (2016). *Collaborative teams that transform schools: The next step in PLCs.* Bloomington, IN: Marzano Research.

Marzano, R. J., Warrick, P., & Simms, J. A. (2014). *A handbook for high reliability schools: The next step in school reform.* Bloomington, IN: Marzano Research.

Marzano, R. J., Waters, T., & McNulty, B. A. (2005). *School leadership that works: From research to results.* Alexandria, VA: Association for Supervision and Curriculum Development.

Mayer, D., & Lloyd, M. (2011). *Professional learning: An introduction to the research literature.* Accessed at http://doereforms.weebly.com/uploads/5/3/5/2/53522887/professional_learning_an_introduction_to_the_research_literature_mayer_-amp-_lloyd_oct_2011.pdf on July 17, 2020.

Morrissey, M. S. (2000). *Professional learning communities: An ongoing exploration.* Accessed at www.allthingsplc.info/files/uploads/plc-ongoing.pdf on 7/17/2020.

Muhammad, A., & Hollie, S. (2012). *The will to lead, the skill to teach: Transforming schools at every level.* Bloomington, IN: Solution Tree Press.

National Center for Literacy Education. (2013). *Remodeling literacy learning: Making room for what works.* Accessed at www.literacyinlearningexchange.org/sites/default/files/ncle_report_final_format_0.pdf on July 17, 2020.

Penlington, C. (2008). Dialogue as a catalyst for teacher change: A conceptual analysis. *International Journal of Research and Studies, 24*(5), 1304–1316.

Pfeffer, J. (2007). *What were they thinking? Unconventional wisdom about management.* Boston: Harvard Business School Press.

Piaget, J. (1973). *To understand is to invent.* New York: Grossman.

Raywid, M. A. (1993). Finding time for collaboration. *Educational Leadership, 51*(1). Accessed at www.ascd.org/publications/educational-leadership/sept93/vol51/num01/Finding-Time-for-Collaboration.aspx on July 17, 2020.

Reeves, D. B. (2004). *Assessing educational leaders: Evaluating performance for improved individual and organizational results.* Thousand Oaks, CA: Corwin Press.

Robinson, V. (2006). Putting education back into educational leadership. *Leading and Managing, 12*(1), 62–75.

Robinson, V., Hohepa, M., & Lloyd, C. (2009). *School leadership and student outcomes: Identifying what works and why.* Ministry of Education (NZ). Accessed at www.educationcounts.govt.nz/__data/assets/pdf_file/0015/60180/BES-Leadership-Web-updated-foreword-2015.pdf on July 17, 2020.

Sahlberg, P. (2011). *Finnish lessons 2.0: What can the world learn from educational change in Finland?* (2nd ed.). New York: Teachers College, Columbia University.

Schein, E. (1992). *Organizational culture and leadership* (2nd ed.). San Francisco: Jossey-Bass.

Sergiovanni, T. J. (1984). Leadership and excellence in schooling: Excellent schools need freedom within boundaries. *Educational Leadership, 41*(5), 4–13.

Sergiovanni, T. J. (2005). *Strengthening the heartbeat: Leading and learning together in schools.* San Francisco: Jossey-Bass.

Sinek, S. (2009). *How great leaders inspire action* [Transcript]. Accessed at www.ted.com/talks/simon_sinek_how_great_leaders_inspire_action/transcript?language=en on July 17, 2020.

Snow-Gerono, J. (2005). Professional development in a culture of inquiry: PDS teachers identify the benefits of professional learning communities. *Teaching and Teacher Education, 21*(3), 241–256.

Tjosvold, D. (1997). Conflict within interdependence: Its value for productivity and individuality. In C. De Dreu & E. Van De Vliert (Eds.), *Using conflict in organizations,* pp. 23–37. Thousand Oaks, CA: Sage.

Trimbur, J. (1992). Consensus and difference in collaborative learning. In P. Shannon (Ed.), *Becoming political: Readings and writings in the politics of literacy education,* pp. 208–222. Portsmouth, NH: Heinemann.

Tschannen-Moran, M. (2004). *Trust matters: Leadership for successful schools.* San Francisco: Jossey-Bass.

Wayman, J. C., Midgley, S., & Stringfield, S. (2006). Leadership for data-based decision making: Collaborative data teams. In A. Danzig, K. Borman, B. Jones, & W. Wright (Eds.), *New models of professional development for learner centered leadership,* pp. 189–206. Mahwah, NJ: Erlbaum.

Weber, C., & Lang-Raad, N. (2015, September 3). *Extreme makeover: RTI edition.* Accessed at www.solutiontree.com/blog/extreme-makeover-rti-edition on July 17, 2020.

Wheelan, S. A. (2013). *Creating effective teams: A guide for members and leaders* (4th ed.). Thousand Oaks, CA: SAGE.

Wiliam, D. (2011). *Embedded formative assessment.* Bloomington, IN: Solution Tree Press.

# INDEX

## Learning by Doing
### *Richard DuFour, Rebecca DuFour, Robert Eaker, Thomas W. Many, and Mike Mattos*

Discover how to transform your school or district into a high-performing PLC. The third edition of this comprehensive action guide offers new strategies for addressing critical PLC topics, including hiring and retaining new staff, creating team-developed common formative assessments, and more.
**BKF746**

## The Big Book of Tools for Collaborative Teams in a PLC at Work®
### *William M. Ferriter*

Build your team's capacity to become agents of change. Organized around the four critical questions of PLC at Work®, this comprehensive resource provides an explicit structure for learning teams. Access tools and templates for navigating common challenges, developing collective teacher efficacy, and more.
**BKF898**

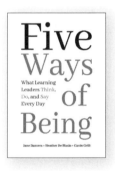

## Five Ways of Being
### *Jane Danvers, Heather De Blasio, and Gavin Grift*

In this must-read guide, the authors challenge and reinvent the mindset of leadership. Each chapter outlines one of five ways of being—from forming trusting relationships to being purposeful in thought and action—that will empower you to genuinely lead learning in staff, colleagues, and students.
**BKB013**

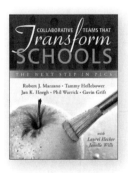

## Collaborative Teams That Transform Schools
### *Robert J. Marzano, Tammy Heflebower, Jan K. Hoegh, Phil Warrick, and Gavin Grift*

Explore research-based steps and strategies you can use to increase the effectiveness of collaborative teams and enhance professional learning communities. Examine how the PLC process can transform critical components of education, including curriculum, assessment, instruction, and teacher development.
**BKL034**

Solution Tree | Press    a division of Solution Tree

Visit SolutionTree.com or call 800.733.6786 to order.

# GLOBAL PD

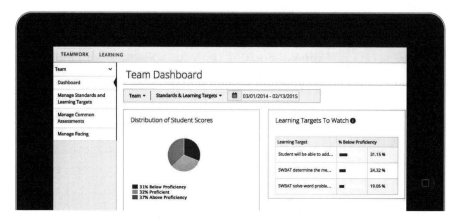

# The **Power to Improve**
## Is in Your Hands

**Global PD** gives educators focused and goals-oriented training from top experts. You can rely on this innovative online tool to improve instruction in every classroom.

- Get unlimited, on-demand access to guided video and book content from top Solution Tree authors.

- Improve practices with personalized virtual coaching from PLC-certified trainers.

- Customize learning based on skill level and time commitments.